Daughters

HOW TO UNTANGLE YOURSELF FROM YOUR MOTHER

JULIA VAUGHAN SMITH

Julia Vaughan Smith
Daughters: How to Untangle Yourself from Your Mother

ISBN paperback: 978-1-3999-4113-6
ISBN ebook: 978-1-3999-4112-9

Names, quotations and examples used in this book do not relate to any living person; they are illustrative only.

This paperback can be ordered from all bookstores as well as from Amazon, and the ebook is available on online platforms such as Amazon and iBooks.

Book Design: Petya Tsankova
Publishing Support: Clapham Publishing Services

"There have been other books on the daughter-mother dynamic but this one is unique in neither demonising nor justifying maternal behaviour. The book provides a calm and penetrating insight into the lasting impact of a daughter's connection with her mother. And if you are personally entangled with your mother, how do you free yourself? Read this astonishing book to find out."

Jenny Rogers, Executive Coach, Author of *'Are you Listening?'*

"This is a wise, elegant and impactful book that sensitively explores the complexity of daughter/mother relationships. With her understanding of emotional trauma, Julia doesn't pull her punches about the devasting impact of some daughter/mother relationships, nor does she vilify mothers. Instead, she shows compassion for the experiences and trauma they may have experienced. Most importantly she offers hope and a means for daughters to shift the relationship dynamics."

Claire Lea, Executive Coach

"If you are struggling to feel loving and giving towards your mother in the way that surely all daughters 'should' this book provides reassurance. You are not alone, abnormal or wicked. Julia points out that a mother is also a daughter. Julia uses her extensive experience as a psychotherapist, coach and daughter to guide us carefully to review our relationship with our mother. She encourages us to take responsibility for our adult selves and explore how our childhood experience may be affecting our adult relationships. This is a hopeful book which you will want to dip into again and again. Julia shows it is never too late to begin to unravel some of our tangled webs and gradually become 'our own good enough loving mother (more of the time)'."

Julia Steward, Leadership Coach, Author of *'Sustaining Resilience for Leadership: Stories from Education'*

"This book is an immensely helpful read. It enables the reader to build a picture of their own life experience alongside those of others. Page by page it sheds light on the shadowy places often found in daughter/mother relationships. It then helps us to work out what to do to understand our lives and, if we choose, to move our relationships onto a healthier positive footing. It is a book you will want to read and reread."

Liz Cleves, Artist

"A book that connects the female universally. Any daughter in the world will be able to find herself in it. Julia comprehensively looks at the female line and the inherited trauma through generations. The book offers an insight into what is our own trauma and which trauma might belong generations before us. Gentle and generous to mothers and very helpful for being a daughter. A way a daughter might heal her difficult relationship with her mother by understanding the relationship between them."

Susanne Gosling, Psychotherapist

For my mother, with love and gratitude

Acknowledgements

I am grateful to all the women I have talked to across the years, and in researching this book, for sharing their stories. Thanks to Jane Krish, Jenny Rogers, Liz Cleves, Brian Lewis, and Alexandra Smith for their valuable comments on my drafts and for the time they took to do that. I am thankful too for the time taken by the other women who read and commented on the book. My gratitude to Lorna Howarth who gave me great editorial advice and input, to all involved in publishing the book and to Sophie Hannah for her advice and guidance. Without the support and encouragement of my husband and friends I may have fallen at the first hurdle, so thank you for helping me press on. Finally, to my mother for all she sacrificed and contributed to enable me to be at this point of my life, with sadness that I can't say that to her directly.

Contents

Preface

Some daughters have joyful relationships with their mothers. Others 'get along alright' without any deep connection or personal angst. If that is your experience, treasure it. Another group are caught up in repetitive cycles of frustration, hostility, criticism, resentment, duty and possibly hatred which leave them exhausted. This group are entangled, that is, caught in a web woven over a lifetime. Within that web, they are stuck. This book is for such daughters, their friends, wider family and others who want to understand the dynamics and how to change.

I have practised as an executive and therapeutic coach for many years and have been a psychotherapist in private practice. In these roles I have listened to many accounts of such entanglements and the lasting impact of them on the inner world of daughters. In preparation for writing this book I talked to a number of women, to whom I am deeply grateful for sharing their stories. I was also an entangled daughter and writing this book has been a heart-felt and personal process for me. At times, this has been challenging as I faced some truths for the first time. Truths about my part in the entanglement as it takes two to create the web. I wanted to give voice to the reality for many daughters and included some of my own reflections to illustrate aspects of differently entangled relationships.

Moving out of entanglement requires us to become aware of, examine and change the patterns of relating that have been built up over our life. If we want to experience things differently, it is down to us. We can't change our mother, if she could be different, she would be. This is a self-coaching book, offering reflective exercises to support you moving out of these repetitive cycles of behaviour, thoughts and feelings. Entanglements drain our energy and become burdensome. If we can stop these patterns, and put healthier ones in place, we are able to live our lives more fully.

You can't change your mother but you can change your inner experience and thoughts

I approach this topic without blame or accusation. Some mothers have caused emotional and physical pain within their daughters and carry responsibility for that behaviour. However, holding onto blame is part of the entanglement, as is holding on to hope that "one day my mother will....". Some whose relationship with their mother is more loving may be surprised that painful and challenging relationships are more common than they might have realised. At the core of entanglement is emotional trauma, passed down through the generations from grandparents, to parents, to children. Understanding what this means for relationships can help us let go of blame, develop compassion for ourselves, and move out of the web.

We may not realise how wounded we are until we have come to a stage in our life when we can acknowledge it

Entanglement is not just created between mothers and daughters, we can become entangled with our fathers, siblings or partners; sons similarly can be entangled with their mothers or fathers. If you are entangled with others, you will find much in this book that is valuable. I focus on that between daughters and mothers

2

specifically, as our mothers are at the centre of our existence. There are many variations in who our 'mothers' are — birth mothers, adoptive mothers, foster mothers, absent mothers, or two mothers who raise us. Fathers may be part of our life or not, if they are they can be a loving or not, able to connect with us or not, or anywhere in between. They too, are important to our psychological growth and to our relationship with our mother and with ourselves. In referring to daughters, I include all who identify with that. There are other complex issues for those who are transgender; however, I hope that much of what I write will be relevant. It is for each of us to enquire within ourselves and explore how our family experience has influenced the entangled relationship with our mother (either birth, adoptive or both) that we want to experience differently.

May this book give you hope that change is possible and the support to help you to make it happen

I hope too, that it will be an interesting and stimulating read for all, including those who are not similarly entangled.

Julia Vaughan Smith

CHAPTER 1
What is Entanglement?

Entanglement describes a relationship that is unsatisfying and often repeatedly hurtful; and yet, despite that, it is one we continually return to and from which we get the same negative outcomes. Why do we stay? The answers are in our deeper emotions from childhood, including a fear of abandonment and the stories we tell ourselves about what staying means.

With our birth mother it starts at conception and the foundations are laid during pregnancy, birth and throughout our childhood with the mother(s) who raised us. From this earliest relationship we develop ideas and thoughts about ourselves; how she responded and talked to us shapes how we think about ourselves. We are like Russian Dolls, nested inside each other. I have a set of such dolls on my windowsill to remind me of this interconnectedness.

It is a form of attachment, or emotional bond, but one that is distorted and doesn't feel loving or fulfilling no matter what we do. Where the daughter:mother relationship is joyful, the emotional bond is present in the pleasure of being together and of having her in our life. In that type of bond there is a sense of a strong connectivity, and the bonds hold us lightly and allow space for us to be who we are. In contrast, where the relationship is difficult or hurtful, the bonds can feel sticky and binding, rather like a spider's web. We can feel stuck in this dysfunctional relationship that makes big demands on us and our individuality, and though we strive to break free, we can't disentangle ourselves. Instead, our wriggling and struggling reinforces those sticky bonds, and thus our suffering.

Our earliest relationships, most significantly for many being with our mother, have a lasting impact on us. Patterns of relating to ourselves and others are established and reverberate throughout our lives. If we felt wanted and loved as a child, we tend to be more loving and honouring towards ourselves and others. If we didn't, we may have problems with our self-esteem and self-belief. The family and life events also shape us and affect how our mother can be with us and how our relationship evolves.

The 'there and then' continues to operate in the 'here and now'

We can be pretty sure that mothers with whom we have difficult and challenging relationships carry their own pain and hurt from early childhood and maybe additionally from adult life experience. We become caught in an emotional trauma system which didn't start with us but with earlier generations. If our ancestors were unable to parent lovingly, for any reason, or who suffered greatly in their lives, it is easy to see how the darker side of mothering (and fathering) can be continued through the generations to us. Our mothers and their mothers will have been affected by their own early life and parents, and the context in which they were born. They will have been affected by the expectations and demands of patriarchal societies on women, and if they question the societal norms they were born into, they were often shamed into silence. Their life experiences have entangled them in unhealthy bonds of their own; they too have suffered and felt alone or afraid.

The 'here and now'

Untangled relationships feel light, bring energy; there is space to be ourselves. There is mutual respect, give and take, and an emotional connection. They are free from 'should, must, have to' thoughts, attention is freely given, and we are not expected to subjugate our lives to hers.

In contrast, the types of behaviour that show themselves within entangled relationships include rescuing, controlling, avoiding, criticising, clinging, dependency, demanding, smothering, self-sacrifice, parenting a parent, being dutiful and wanting to please. The emotions involve fear, anxiety, hurt, anger, frustration, exasperation, feeling responsible and possibly hatred. The behaviour from the mother may include negativity, rejection, or distancing, clinging dependency, putting her own needs before anyone else, giving the impression nothing ever being enough for her, or she may be absent physically or emotionally. The entanglements arise through the daughter trying to feel love, to be seen and respected and from adapting to the behaviour of her mother.

The more typical complicated and difficult relationships and established patterns between daughters and their mothers include:

The dutiful but resentful daughter

The daughter does what she believes she 'ought to do', with a sense of obligation. What gets lost is loving connection. The resentment may arise if what is done is taken for granted or is never enough. It is a commonly felt emotion in all entangled relationships.

The rescuer and protector

Rescuing and protecting are ways we can tell ourselves 'we are being helpful', however, we often end up feeling resentful and at the same time prevent our mother making her own decisions.

The daughter as parent

Some mothers have depended on partners for a lot of their life, not taking adult responsibility for themselves. If they become single, the mother may turn to the daughter requiring her to take up the adult responsibility. The daughter takes on this role through duty or a desire to get her mother's love or because she feels responsible.

The responsible daughter

The daughter feels responsible for her mother's life and wellbeing; this maybe towards a mother who is dependent and who is unable to take responsibility for herself or her life decisions. It is a form of rescuing.

The self-sacrificing daughter
All of the above could be self-sacrificing, that is, the daughter puts her own life and needs away and focuses on meeting her mother's expressed needs no matter the impact on the daughter's life.

The daughter who feels smothered
This might look loving from outside, as there seems to be a lot of contact and involvement from the mother. However, what is happening is that the mother sees no boundaries between her and her daughter when it comes to interfering in her daughter's life or decisions.

The distanced daughter
The distance may be one kept by the mother, emotionally and/or physically; daughters can respond to this in ways that keep them entangled. A symptom of entanglement may be that the daughter keeps her mother emotionally or physically distant as a way of trying to protect herself. While this provides her some refuge, it hasn't broken the entanglement which may be reignited when contact is made.

The hurt and silent daughter
Some mothers criticise and emotionally hurt their daughters repeatedly, and have done since childhood, and the daughter takes it all on remaining silent about the hurt she feels.

The angry and hating daughter
If our mother has treated us badly for a much of our life, our anger and hatred can grow and consume us. In an entanglement it becomes the focus of all our narratives about our mother. Re-

telling these stories over and over rarely resolves it, but tightens the web even tighter. Anger can lead us to protect ourselves from another who violates our boundaries; that is healthy. But in entanglement it has become 'chronic', always present, unresolved with nowhere to go.

Entanglement is distorted love towards our mother and ourselves

These relationships are not mutually exclusive, nor are they comprehensive. You may describe your entanglement, if you are in one, in a different way. I expand them all with more detail in Part 2 and you can explore what resonates with you in relation to your experience. Many of us have had ill and aging mothers and have wanted to provide care and support to them. It is entirely possible to do that in ways that are unentangled as I describe in Part 4.

Any of these types of relationships could have their roles swapped with the mother being the rescuer, or feeling over responsible for her adult daughter, or feeling hurt and silenced by her daughter's criticism, or experiencing her daughter as cold and distant. The daughter may be the one not taking adult responsibility for herself. The daughter may have a long term health condition where more input from the mother is needed, but it doesn't have to become an entangled relationship just because there is a care-taking function.

The 'there and then'

To understand our relationship with our mother, we need to revisit the beginning of our connection with her and the context of our early life together. At the same time, we need to recognise our own uniqueness, our own personality and inner engagement with life. The nature/nurture debate has long been around; whatever the balance between the two there is clear evidence that how we are nurtured has a major influence on us. And it makes sense that there is also a nature component to our genetic makeup that affects how we respond to experiences. Our unique engagement with life helps us find imaginative ways to adapt to and survive our environments. Some childhood experiences can diminish that energy within us—that drive to be ourselves—but it never goes away; it is always there, waiting for the opportunity to become fully ourselves.

How it affects our inner world

We take in and create ideas about ourselves from how those emotionally nearest to us, our mothers and other close care givers, behave towards us. These thoughts and feelings affect how we relate to her, to ourselves and to others. As children, we understand little of what is going on around us but we try to make sense of it. It rarely crosses our mind that it is anything other than our fault; the thinking may be *'if they act as if they don't love or value me, it must be because of how I am'.* For example, we may think and believe:
- I am not good enough/lovable
- I must please everyone (or I won't be loved)
- I am too demanding/needy/strong willed

Beneath these thoughts is our fear of being abandoned. As children we are totally dependent with nowhere else to go. We survive emotionally and psychologically the best we can.

The dark side of mothering

The illusion of the all-loving mother is a myth. Fairy-tales tell us there is a darker side to mothering. Sit and listen to daughters (and sons) and hear their experience of how a mother's behaviour can be unloving, emotionally damaging and sometimes physically painful. We can understand this in the context of the mother's experience and how she has been treated by society and the often unreasonable expectations placed on women to be mothers AND to be all-loving. It is almost impossible for women to talk about negative feelings towards their children, out of fear about how they will be viewed. But for some mothers, there is an ambivalence about pregnancy and being a mother, or of being a mother of this child right now. I use the term 'the dark side of mothering' to capture this and to challenge the myth; it is part of the reality of mothering and of being a child. We need to engage with this without blame or shame as neither will help us become unentangled.

Supporting learning and change

We can all become curiously enquiring of our own web and the patterns within it. We can observe the densely knotted parts, those bits where all the dust has collected because they have been undisturbed for so long. We can also find, experience, and enjoy those parts of our web where love, compassion and creativity lie. We can reflect on those aspects we might want to expand and nurture and those aspects that we wish to change, and perhaps how to explore our webs with those nearest us.

If you recognise that you want to change your tangled web, this book will support you in that. To begin with, you can set yourself the intention of becoming aware of your part in keeping it going, because undoubtedly, we all play a role in perpetuating the status quo. During the changes you undertake, there are bound to be setbacks and at times it might feel like one step forward and two steps backwards, but this is what change is like.

Personal enquiry isn't a linear process, it is more like a spiral where we find ourselves facing similar issues time and again, ones we thought we had already resolved. But, we are not back at the same place; we are coming to the issue with the learning and insight we had from the last time we engaged with those issues. In Celtic tradition there is the symbol of the Triple Spiral (the 'triskelion' or 'triskel') which has many different symbolic meanings, one of which is that it represents the various phases of womanhood, from maiden, through maturity (and motherhood for some) then wise woman.

The three parts could be seen as our relationship with our mother, with ourselves, and as women or people in this world. This is the process we are moving through as we take up this call to change for ourselves.

Making Space for Reflection

Many of us live busy lives, trying to juggle many things. Into that comes our relationship with our mother, which may take time we feel we don't have and which may be unrewarding. To disentangle ourselves we need time to reflect on our encounters with our mother, and the context in which our relationship evolved. We need to slow our lives down so we can reflect and digest our emotional responses and to explore what thoughts or beliefs may be behind our actions. We need to create space to raise our self-awareness and expand our understanding of the dynamics we are co-creating.

Deciding to act

We will need to take different actions at many points of our exploration and change process. We each need to decide what we are committed to, what our intention is and what action we want to take. Remember, we are doing this for ourselves, not for anyone else. We may need to shake off apathy in deciding to take action. Deciding isn't about 'shoulds' or 'musts' but needs to come from clear choice and commitment to ourselves. Maybe your first decision has been to read this book and to see what, if any, other decisions you want to take.

Let go of blame Let go of blame Let go of blame

Holding onto blame can keep us stuck, it prevents us finding our way out of the tangled web. As long as those we blame remain the focus of our attention, nothing will change. Shifting the blame to ourselves means still to be entangled. We need to focus our attention on ourselves. This isn't selfish, it is about honouring yourself and your processes of change.

No longer blaming our mother for the pain she may have caused us does not imply she is beyond reproach nor that she doesn't carry responsibility for her behaviour. We need to be able to hold our pain tenderly, while also engaging with how we may be adding to our own suffering. So many of our responses to our mother, ourselves and others, come from the adaptations and contortions we had to make as children. If we engage our capacity for reflection and compassion, we can explore these habits and adjustments without judgement and begin to see our patterns more clearly.

Developing the capacity for self-calming

We are often primed to become agitated in response to certain conditions; maybe the way our mother speaks curtly to us or responds in predictable patterns that bring hurt or anger. That agitation can spill over into the rest of our lives, for example, in our work relationships. As children we learnt how to calm ourselves by the way others calmed us when we were frightened or anxious. Many mothers were not able to model that for their daughters because they hadn't learnt how to calm themselves as children or later as adults. As a result, many of us tend to experience agitation and anxiety more often than is healthy for us. It is useful for us to learn and practise techniques that build a quality of calmness in our lives and the ability to reassure ourselves. Part of this is being able to identify, name, and have compassion for the feelings we have, whatever they are.

Finding and using support

If you recognise that you are caught in a sticky web of relationships, you may know what it is to feel alone with your hurt, and you may have carried that pain for a long time. You may have learnt as a child that asking for help doesn't work, because when you reached out to those closest to you early in life, you didn't get the help and support needed. You might have been rejected or told you were wrong to ask or were given 'help' that wasn't what you wanted. Many of us learnt that reaching out to another doesn't always bring the warmth we were seeking. It can be testing for some adult daughters to seek and ask for help. It can feel difficult, and we can feel ashamed of our need for support.

However, the process of changing the effect our mother has on us, and old patterns of thinking and behaving, will be aided if we have support from others who care about us or are professional practitioners. The support might come from close and trusted friends, from development and therapeutic groups, or from a therapist or coach. It might take a while to find the best support for you; however, you will find it if you keep yourself open to the possibility that it is somewhere waiting for you.

Raising your self-awareness

No matter what sort of relationship web we feel part of, raising our self-awareness is always fundamental to progress. This requires us to develop our capacity for self-reflection and self-enquiry. Curiosity, compassion and lack of judgement are our aids here; to be curious about ourself, our thoughts and feelings, about what is going on in our 'inner being', whilst giving ourselves loving support. This is about connecting our responses in the 'here and now' to our associations from the 'there and then'. There may be many factors to explore, and each time we engage with enquiry something else might emerge, a sense or memory or feeling that comes from an earlier age. The more we bring things into conscious awareness we have different choices available. What remains unconscious comes out in negative ways that can be harmful to us and to others.

Some people find writing a Reflective Journal is a good way to help this self-processing. My notes at the beginning of each chapter come from my reflective journal. Journaling in this way is about writing to process thoughts, feelings, images and experiences. It is not writing for anyone else and indeed, having written something on one day, we might never go back and read it again. Its purpose is not to be a record, it is to support our exploration, in private, with ourselves. Ten to thirty minutes a day, or several times a week can be helpful. Sit quietly, with a notebook and a pen you love to use, and just write about your thoughts and feelings. Ask yourself questions and answer them. For example, you might start with taking some deep breaths and connecting with your body. Then you can ask yourself questions like, *'What am I experiencing or feeling in my body?'*; *'What is uppermost in my* awareness? *(It might be an argument, or misunderstanding, or a memory – anything that arises); 'Where do I feel strong in my body and where do I feel weaker?'* Or you can just write freely, allowing whatever comes up to spill from your pen, noticing what arises within you, going deeper into yourself, your motivations, your feelings and thoughts. Catch the thoughts and write them down. Look at them and explore, *'Are they true?; 'Are they helpful to me?'* and *'What might be beneath them?'* You will all come to this process in your own ways – there is no right or wrong way to do this. Just start, engage with reflective learning and see where it takes you.

You can also use the Reflective Journal to write about situations that happen. You can set out what happened, how you felt, what you were thinking and what the outcome was. You can write about how you might have had a different outcome, assuming the one you had was not a positive one. If it was positive, you can reflect on what enabled that to happen? In this way we deepen our learning.

Honouring your experience

Carrying illusions about our childhood can keep us feeling relatively safe and certainly loyal, however, it doesn't help us change an unhealthy relationship web. Some people have closed off their awareness to the reality of their experiences, wanting to pretend that all was 'great' and that they had a happy childhood. If this was your real experience, treasure it. Often though, daughters pretend they did, while knowing deep inside themselves that they did not. It is about choosing to honour ourselves and our experiences, without blame or recrimination. I hear many daughters dismiss their experience as *'nothing'* or that *'many others had it much harder than me'*. It is never 'nothing', and the intensity of experience is not in question; it is the effects of that experience that is.

Many worry that acknowledging the reality of our childhood experiences may make things worse, and whilst it is important to take good care of ourselves and take slow steps towards the goal of disentangling from any dysfunctional webs, it is unlikely that things will get worse, because you are not apportioning blame – you are reflecting on the reality of what was. Therefore, do this work in your own time, when it feels possible for you, maybe with the support of professional therapy practitioner. You must choose how much reality you can face, and when.

Compassion and love

We have the option to become our own loving mother, developing an inner capacity to love, cherish and nurture ourselves. For some, this isn't easy, as we have internalised the negative voices from early life and maybe have come to a deeply held belief that we are not lovable. This can only be countered by stronger loving energy for yourself. It can be one of the most challenging steps – to love yourself and to have compassion for yourself especially when you make mistakes or fail yourself in some way. It is often much easier to be kind and generous hearted to others than to yourself as you have taken in so much negative talk and ideas about yourself. Nonetheless, we have to learn to love ourselves.

It is also about being kind and recognising that our mother has suffered too, that she has felt pain and fear, and that we can engage with her humanity while not accepting her treatment of us. 'Kind' does not mean accommodating how she is with us; it is about how we express our needs and our boundaries.

You may choose to read this book from the beginning to the end or start where your attention takes you and work outwards from there. You can do the exercises as you go along, go back to them or ignore them, whatever works best for you to get what you want from this book. If you find some sections stimulate some distress within you, put the book aside, go and do something that is resourcing to you or talk to someone, that is part of shifting out of entanglement.

As I said, some of us need help to take these steps. I have been greatly supported by wise therapy, good friends and a loving partner. We all need help in whatever form it takes; like a spider's web, our emotional web is very resilient, having been in place for a long time. As we become familiar with our unique web and recognise that parts of it are similar to other mother/daughter webs, we can experiment with different patterns of thinking and behaving. In particular, how to stop repeated, debilitating exchanges with our mother, if she is still alive; how to change the way we talk and think about ourselves; and how to change our habitual responses to others. The answers are within us, not within our mother. We can't change her. Once we really understand that and stop making her the centre of our inner world, we can make progress.

PART 1

CHILDHOOD: WHERE IT ALL STARTS

Personal Reflection (1)

As I begin writing about our stories, I notice a split in myself: the part that sees my mother and feels compassion for her and has memories of her kindness and generosity, and the part that is still deeply troubled from the relationship. The challenge is to hold both of these parts so that one doesn't obliterate the other. I know some daughters will not have many, if any, memories of kindness from their mother yet may have seen her be kind to others, which is doubly painful; some will have lots of good memories.

I've noticed at times a struggle between different aspects of myself. There's a part of me that has clarity and knows what it wants to say, then there is a part full of self-doubt and anxiety about saying it. That part feels silenced by my internal critic, she who crushes my creativity. My internal critic has learnt to do this over many years as she believes it keeps me safe. I now realise this is an illusion, but I want to treasure her care for me.

I know I am pushing against the story – the myth – we are supposed to tell about our mothers; how wonderful and self-sacrificing they are, how grateful we are to have them in our lives. Part of me fears not being believed or taken seriously, or more devastatingly, that I am wrong or will be proved wrong. It is hard to believe your voice will be valued and heard when as a child it often wasn't. Some of the stories I tell are diverse and challenge the mythology of motherhood. I think my internal critic doesn't want me to tell these truths, maybe because some of it is shameful or could expose others.

This leads me to think about the idea of 'the feminine' from the world of archetypes and goddesses. The feminine archetype is often represented by the idea of the 'Great Mother,' the all-loving mother who is associated with abundance, nurturing and fertility. I once recoiled at a workshop where we were invited to seek out and welcome in this 'Mother'. There was no mention of the 'shadow side' of this archetype— the mother that can kill off, poison, reject or smother her children. This is the shadow side of mothering which the myth tries to silence.

CHAPTER 2
Your Earliest Connection with Your Mother

For the majority of us, our relationship with our mother starts physiologically even before we are conceived. The egg that created us was in her body when she was in her own mother's womb. Half the essence of us has therefore travelled with her from her beginning. This means that we are connected with our grandmother from the start of our own mother's life. Our grandmother's life situation and psychology impacted our mother and us, and then our mother's situation also affected us, and on it goes. We have been linked together by the relational web for longer than we might imagine.

For others, our relationship might start before we even meet physically, for example in egg donation. In egg donation and IVF, mothers will have been through many treatment hoops before becoming pregnant and the baby is already in her imagination. If our history is that of being the result of an egg donation, we became physiologically connected from the time we become embedded in the wall of the womb. Our mother's history becomes ours as we develop within her. The donor of the egg is also in our system through the DNA that it carries.

Most birth mothers continue to raise their children or stay proactive in their lives. Sometimes another mother may come into our lives through need, perhaps adoption, fostering or as a stepmother. Sometimes a grandmother or father will step into that role. This person becomes our mother with whom we develop an emotional bond, while retaining that short early connection with our birth mother. The attachment could become entangled with either or both, including if the birth mother exited our lives.

This is where the relationship web begins and it continues to be woven by us with our mother, through infancy and childhood. It is influenced by our immature nervous system responses to stressors in the environment; and core to this environment is our mother (or mothers). If we feel wanted, safe and loved, our stress levels remain low and we are able to engage freely and without fear of those around us. The relationship bond develops as a loving, holding connection, the essence of which remains with us into adulthood. However, if our mother, others, or the environment we find ourselves in, stimulates our immature stress responses producing fear, we become anxious for our safety and are unable to meet our own needs for security. We tend to hang on emotionally and this can create the entangled, sticky web that continues to evolve and linger into adulthood. The web develops as a way to calm our agitated nervous system and to manage the fear of abandonment.

Our unique relational web with our mother is about the two of us, within the family system and culture of which we are a part –

even if we have siblings. Our siblings will have a different relational web to us. The web is influenced by our mother's emotional state, by the relationships we both have around us and how loving and safe that experience is for both of us. As infants we pick up on our mother-figure's emotional wellbeing. If she is relaxed and happy with us enough of the time, then we absorb those energies and feel wanted and loved; if she attends to us but not with love, not with a smile, then we feel stressed and anxious. We are also highly sensitive to being separated from her. If she or we had to go into hospital, or she was ill and couldn't care for us, we would have felt her loss as being life threatening, even if those caring for us might have done so lovingly.

If during pregnancy a mother is stressed and not supported, those stress hormones pass into the child. If she doesn't want to be pregnant that is sensed by the child's immature brain. Mothers and daughters share a birth process that can be straightforward or might have complications and bring high stress to them both. Some births that don't go as the mother hoped, for example a caesarean rather than a 'natural' birth, may cause her to feel she has failed her daughter in some way. With complicated births, mother and child have shared an experience that could have had life-long consequences for both. Motherhood is a potentially stressful time for many. This can be reduced if the family context and parental partnership is loving and protecting of the mother and baby, if there is enough money to live on and there is joy and laughter in the family. But some mothers find themselves with little support, if any, either because no other family members are around, or because those who are do not provide the emotional and physical protection that is needed.

Such experiences are part of life, which is why emotional trauma and complex relationships with our mothers are part of the human condition. A difficult adult relationship between a daughter and her mother is likely to have its roots in these early years. For some it might be very early, for others it might be that the nature of the relationship changed as we moved from being an infant to a toddler to a child, and when we were developing our own personality.

What is expected of mothers – by which I mean how they are 'supposed' to care for their babies – is largely culturally determined. The pressures and expectations on them can be huge and if they step out of line the disapproval can be great. Each generation has its version of 'how to be the best mother'. Not all of these approaches have a positive impact on the baby; some of them create stress and anxiety. For example, the now out of date advice to feed the baby only every four hours whether she is hungry or not. Often, she is likely to be ravenous and in need of food much sooner; at other times she might not be hungry but is expected to eat. At one time, not so long ago, the received wisdom was to leave babies to cry, so they learn that they can't always be picked up. However, many children learn to stop crying out of despair, not because they have learnt to reassure themselves, which again can have life-long consequences. Conversely, always carrying the baby around might create a close bond, but at some time the child needs to learn about their separateness from their mother-figure. Good parenting is not easy and is full of conundrums.

Depending on your age, and the experience of your mother in caring for her offspring, you are likely to have been subjected to whatever was the cultural childcaring imperative at the time. Mothers who follow these fashions – whether through peer pressure or because they do not recognise or trust their own mothering instincts – do so because they want to do the best for their children. It is not the mother's motivation though that affects the baby – it is the behaviour and the quality of the contact. Babies can't think things through, they react on the level of feeling safe and protected, or not.

There are many other pressures on mothers from society that may stimulate shame in them and create emotional distance from their daughters. These will vary depending on the nature of the community into which the baby is born, and the customs and practices that are passed on. It might be that the mother continues to believe that these practices are the right thing to do, though other mothers will decide for themselves how they wish to mother their daughter. Breastfeeding is an example of where mothers can be conflicted. It is high on the agenda of 'What Women Should Do', for all the reasons we understand, but this can make it distressing for women who struggle with breastfeeding, or for those who find it challenging to have this level of intimacy with their baby. Such a mother may well continue to breastfeed but develop resentment towards the baby's hunger; or give up and feel ashamed that she has failed because of the ideal held up to her. She may blame herself or the baby, neither of which is healthy. Consequently, she may believe she is a bad mother, which is shaming and will have a ripple effect throughout her early mothering. She isn't a bad mother; it is societal pressure making her believe she is. At the same time, her baby will have picked up on the tension and felt her mother pull away in the pain. The baby will feel this as potentially dangerous to her survival.

It is not the mother's motivation that affects the baby – it is the behaviour and the quality of the contact

Some mothers who had difficult childhood experiences may find themselves in challenging relationships and circumstances. Others may have problems with addiction or with their mental health. As a result, some mothers may find it hard to connect lovingly and consistently with their baby; as a result, they may not touch or cuddle the baby much, and they might shy away from too much intimacy; or they may not be able to engage in playful interaction. For example, nappy changing can become a task to be completed quickly, rather than an opportunity for loving connection. Being held lovingly is important for a child's sense of safety, and playful interaction and stimulation are necessary for brain development and for building up a 'sense of self'. Many mothers can do this, but others can't. The result can be that daughters feel unloved and unseen and may grow up thinking that they weren't lovable enough.

How a mother behaves with her daughter, therefore, has a major impact on the daughter's development and how the relationship evolves. The following scenarios illustrate how this starts early in our lives and can either result in a continuum of closeness where healthy bonding is maintained, or where the opposite occurs.

A Continuum of Closeness

Scenario 1

Imagine seeing a film of a daughter with a mother who loves her, who takes a lot of joy in her and encourages her to find out who she is. In this film they may be sitting closely, able to look into each other's eyes, and touch each other lovingly; maybe the daughter is sitting on her mother's lap feeling safely held. The soundtrack has soft voices, light tones and giggling from the daughter. The little girl looks safe and relaxed, as does the mother; they delight in each other's company.

Scenario 2

This time, imagine a scene where the daughter and mother might be in the same room, but the mother is focused on something else and ignores her baby daughter. The daughter might keep trying to get her mother's attention but fails or gets a sharp-toned response. There is no laughter. The daughter looks lonely and anxious. There was a 'blank face' experiment done in around 2007 where the mother first plays and engages lovingly with her six-month old baby. Then the mother turns away and comes back to face the baby with a blank face and silent. The baby does all she can to get the mother's attention back. Eventually she goes silent herself; she is confused and her stress responses kick-in. I find it almost too painful to watch. While this is an experiment, similar situations may arise if the mother is preoccupied or depressed or has too many other demands on her time and attention. This isn't a mother being intentionally hurtful, just one juggling too many things. It might happen occasionally or be symptomatic of the relationship as a whole. Some mothers find it hard to emotionally connect with their baby and she is experienced by the child as distant and cold.

Scenario 3

For this third scene, imagine a mother who is out of control emotionally, and is shouting either at her daughter or at another in the daughter's presence. Or, where the mother herself is scared of a violent partner, who is the one out of control. The daughter is likely to be terrified herself and possibly crying, or in a shocked silence as she has learnt that crying draws attention to herself and she may be punished for it. Imagine how the daughter might hold herself: she is likely to be tense, hardly daring to breathe, her body rigid; she might hide behind the sofa or run to another room and shut herself away. Fear may make her feel 'frozen' or numb as the stress hormones gather within her. She senses there is no protection for her and is very afraid. Her mother has turned into a different type of person, who is almost unrecognisable; or her father (or whoever the aggressor is) has similarly changed and she senses her mother's fear. She is trapped. Later, or the next day, the aggressor has changed again, into a calmer person, who expects the relationship to return to how it was before the anger. The daughter might cling to this person, hoping to stop it happening again, only for the terror to be repeated another time. Or the daughter might hold herself distant, or when she is older, learn how to pretend everything is OK; trying to live with these contractions of love and violence.

The difference between these three scenarios is the extent to which the child looks and feels safe, wanted and loved. Being a daughter can be full of love and joy, with a mother who encourages her to live fully. Their bond may be close, where the daughter feels both emotionally held and free to be herself. Many of us carry a fantasy about ideal mothers and fathers, creating a drama in our minds about 'what might have been' as a way of distracting ourselves from what is and was.

For some daughters there may have been times of closeness and warmth, mixed in with times when there was a complete lack of it. For others, life was colder and emptier a lot of the time. Perhaps there was a loving father, grandmother or aunt who was able to offer something our mother was unable to; maybe we had siblings who provided a loving connection with us and with whom we could share our experiences – and whilst these relationships don't change our primary relationship with our mother, they may have a resonance in our relationship with ourselves and contribute to our internal resourcefulness.

Each child in the family will have had a different experience of being mothered, which will have its own unique set of consequences, good and less so. No two sisters have the same mothering experience. Our position in the family order, the context at the time of conception and later during early childhood, together with the genetic inheritance of each of us, makes our daughter experience unique. Therefore, if we have a sister or sisters, there may be some similarities in how our emotional bonding presents but we are each likely to have a different relationship with our mother and with ourselves. One daughter might experience a close relationship with her mother, while another may feel unwanted or unloved. If there is a brother, he might become the 'apple of mother's eye' and all her attention goes to him, leaving the daughter(s) feeling left out. We each learn how to adapt to the mothering we receive in our own way and therefore, siblings weave differently entangled webs.

No two sisters have the same mothering experience

In step-families where there are step- and half-sibling relationships, the step-mother's interactions are likely to vary across the daughters, as for any mother. There are likely to be subtle or not so subtle ways in which she treats them differently and this will not always be that her own children are favoured. A daughter might get 'lost' in a complicated family of siblings, half-siblings and step-siblings, where different needs exist and the mother tries to respond the best she can. There are more of these blended families in recent generations, many of which are successful and happy. Yet even with a loving step-mother, finding one's place in a family with such complicated relationships is hard for any child.

As we become toddlers, children, and then adolescents we present different joys and challenges for our mothers. Some mothers will relish seeing a daughter developing her own persona; at times no doubt also finding it demanding and frustrating. Other daughters may have mothers who demand, through control and punishment (subtle or not), that we become the daughter they want us to be, which is not necessarily who we are. We may be expected to dress in a certain way or behave in rather restrictive ways such as sitting still or keeping clean. A mother may criticise her daughter for how she looks, or what she does, or for making her life difficult. We might be her favourite child or know that we definitely are not. Our mother may have been demanding, jealous, and/or self-absorbed and seemingly impossible to satisfy some, or all, of the time. She might have hated us at times, and we might have seen that in her eyes. As young children we learnt how to adapt to stay in any kind of emotional contact because we had no choice. In doing so, however, we lost some vital connections with our growing selves and with our own life energy. The good news is that we can find ways of reconnecting with that as adults.

We are all on a continuum of closeness. Some daughters will be nearer the 'loving' end of the spectrum, and some will be nearer the middle, experiencing some closeness and some disconnection. Those with the most tangled webs are huddled towards the other end of the spectrum and are caught in unsatisfying and painful cycles of relating. A close, loving relationship is one that is relaxed, fun, respectful and emotionally engaged. Some closeness and disconnection means that at times it can be a loving relationship and then really difficult and challenging. We learn to adapt to the parents we have for our own survival, but these adaptations form an entangled, sticky web that affects our adult relationship, most especially with our mother and with ourselves.

Those who experience a loving relationship with their mother may not realise that some mothering is very different. No mother is super-human – they all have times when they are impatient, frustrated and distracted. However, for some daughters, their mother's behaviour wasn't transiently detached; it was consistently and predictably detached, and for these daughters, the relational web becomes tangled and love is distorted. Part 3 of this book explores some of these issues in greater depth.

Spiral of Learning

- Where would you place yourself on the Continuum of Closeness as a child in relation to your birth mother and/or the person you relate to as mother?

Loving, close, safe   *Distorted, unloved, unsafe*

_____

Did this change over your childhood and adult life? If so in what ways? If in a positive direction what facilitated that change?
  - *Who was around with whom you had a loving connection?*
  - *Imagining your relational web with the person you related to as mother, and with your birth mother if different?*
  - *What is your relational web or bond like with your birth mother? Maybe an image or phrase comes to mind with "it's a bit like...". Perhaps it is the emotions you feel. Remember to include the positives where they exist.*
  - *If you were to create a web, would it be made up with wool or string, rope or silk ribbons – or something else?*
  - *Would your web have lots of colour or be grey and dull?*
  - *Which memories might carry colour, if any?*
  - *Would your web have any gems or other items woven into it?*

If imagining in this way is difficult, list some words that capture the essence of the web as you experience it. Maybe start with 'it feels like'....
  - *As you imagine this web that you have woven over the years, what would you like to change?*

CHAPTER 3
Family Dynamics and How They Affect Us

While this book focuses on the relationship between daughters and our mothers, other early relationships and the family play a significant part in how we become who we are. Nestled in the family dynamics is our relationship with our mother, father and/or other parent, and siblings. It's where we witness and learn about our parent's relationships with their parents. Family dynamics are how the family operates and the conscious and unconscious rules, expectations and roles fulfilled that underpin that. These will include what is acceptable or not, what can be talked about, how feelings and emotional experience are processed, what is expected of children and who holds the power. How families work as a unit is affected by class and ethnicity, and religion if that plays a part. All families are unique, although we often grow up thinking ours is typical of many.

Beside our mother, the other significant relationship is with our father, be that birth-, step- or adoptive. As with mothers, the birth father may or may not play a large part in our life and another may become our father or another mother. Our connection with him, or our other parent, might be loving and holding or the opposite, or anywhere in between. They might be a big presence in our life or peripheral. We create a different web of attachment with them. My father was very important in my life as a child, although, as was the trend then, I didn't see much of him. Many fathers now have a much more hands-on role in childcare and therefore have become more of a central figure in a daughter's life. Maybe we grew up in a single parent household, as I did from the age of nine, where our mother or father is holding the family together.

If our relationship with our mother is poor, daughters may turn to their father or other parent for the closeness they seek, possibly from an early age. If the daughter is unable to connect emotionally with the mother and turns to the father, the father may reinforce this treating his daughter as a special person in his life. Mothers may become jealous of this relationship, putting more distance between her and her daughter. A daughter who responded in this way may have unconsciously or intentionally wanted to shut her mother out. These factors remain within her adult relationship with her mother and may influence some of her adult relationships with men and women. Conversely, many daughters can have a close relationship with both their mother and their father/other parent and there is no competition or need to seek emotionally closeness with one over the other.

Most people are part of an extended family of grandparents, uncles, aunts, cousins and siblings. This may be a dynamic, talkative family that interacts, often providing wonderfully warm and emotionally coherent experiences, or it may feel chaotic and confusing, or one where the family is small and not very outgoing. Some daughters spend their early years in children's homes or in care, with the insecurity of that situation, experiencing instability whenever there is a change of carers. All family experiences are different. Whatever the type of family you were born into, large or small, extensive or not, your particular family dynamic will always have an impact.

Our mother is affected by the family she may have joined through marriage or her relationship. We will all have heard of women who found their 'new' family difficult to interact with, or that the family appeared to think she was not worthy of her partner. Such a situation may cause the mother to be anxious and to feel unsupported at times. Her daughter will be affected by these undercurrents that she can sense but can't understand.

Family systems therapy is a branch of psychotherapy that takes the focus away from one-on-one relationship dynamics and instead attends to the family as a whole entity. Each family has its own unwritten rules, unconscious expectations, beliefs and biases that underpin the inter-relationships. We learn what they are, and as children, we know that we must abide by them for fear of expulsion or abandonment. These rules and expectations affect how communication happens and the level of emotional contact and processing that is 'allowed'. They also shape the roles of the mother and father, and how child rearing is handled. This might sit well with our mother, or she may feel pushed in how she is expected to be a 'mother'.

Sometimes daughters may find a way into another family – that of friends perhaps – to escape theirs and in an attempt to find a culture that feels more accepting of them. I noticed in my interviews that several of us had done that, including those of us who had a parent who had died.

Each family has its own unwritten rules, unconscious expectations, beliefs and biases that underpin the inter-relationships

The Emotional thermostat

Families have different 'emotional thermostats'. Some are fiery, where emotions run high with both joy and anger and the family knows how to be comfortable with that; no one is victimised by the anger. Other families may be cooler, where emotions are rarely expressed or processed, and communication tends to be quiet or more subdued. I was part of a small, rather isolated family, with a low emotional thermostat.

Within family systems thinking, family members are unconsciously assigned and take up roles to help maintain the system. Some of these include 'the scapegoat', the member who is blamed for most things that negatively affect the family; the 'martyr', who suffers for the family, sacrificing herself, and who often makes the family aware of this fact; 'the pseudo-parent', the child who takes on a parental role; the 'problem solver'; the 'rescuer' (usually of mother); the 'protector' (of a parent or sibling); 'mother's little helper'; 'daddy's girl', she who becomes his favourite; and 'the diplomat', the one who calmly facilitates negotiations between family members. All these roles help to keep the family's 'emotional thermostat' at the chosen ambient temperature.

Sometimes a child is allocated the role of the 'favoured' or the 'least favoured' child, even if parents strongly deny they have a favourite. Being the favoured child can give some benefits but can be experienced as stifling and difficult. If the mother is critical or demanding a daughter may have taken on the role of mother's little helper which often brings favouritism together with praise and a sense of connection but over time and as the child grows up, can become a huge burden. There is no guarantee that being given the role of the favoured one will continue; if the energy to maintain it diminishes as it often does, the mother might decide that the daughter is now the 'lease favourite' and even 'uncaring'. The loss of status of this role can be both a relief and devastating.

A daughter may take on the role of the 'lightning rod' being the one who picks up on the unexpressed and unprocessed emotions within a family. They may be described as over-sensitive, which enables the issue to be located in the daughter, rather than in the family system itself. In some families where there are complex and repressed family dynamics, a child may become the one who presents as troubled and unhappy, or depressed and anxious. This may bring them more attention, but the child becomes the problem the family focuses on, rather than on the quality of relating, interacting and emotion-processing that goes on. If we have taken on such a role as a child, it is likely that we keep it as we get older – not always, but often.

Relationship dynamics

Parents as a couple have their own emotional and sexual relationship which excludes their children. This is healthy for their relationship unless it is so exclusive that the children are experienced as an unwelcome interruption. If that is the case, a child may feel unwanted. Whether the parental relationship is strong and loving, or conflicted and unloving, it is felt throughout the family. All adult relationships have challenges, and some break down. The loss of a parent through separation or divorce is hard enough, but often made harder for the children by the hurt and anger that can be released into the family system. Where this is the case, as children we are already grieving the loss of the parent, within a situation which is largely outside our understanding and totally outside our influence, and the remaining parent is caught up in their own pain and is emotionally unavailable to us. The child also now has two family systems to negotiate, which can be entirely different in nature and can be confusing and leave the child feeling like an outsider in one or both, unable to determine the temperature of the emotional thermostat.

How a family system holds them together can be a profound bonding experience between siblings, producing either a closeness that lasts into adulthood, or sibling rivalry, as siblings are compared or put in competition with each other. Children will jostle for the emotional contact they crave or withdraw into themselves. Siblings can bully and abuse each other, sometimes even sexually, and often such bullying and abuse is not dealt with by the parents, or the 'victim' is blamed while the bully is protected. Children can feel betrayed by this, and trust in their parents will be diminished. If the parental relationship is poor or conflicted, this is often mirrored in splits and conflicts between the children.

Safety at home

Many family systems and homes are safe places to grow up in, and even if the emotional thermostat is turned up to maximum and there are occasional outbursts of anger, those involved can come to a resolution and there is no lasting emotional damage and no physical harm done. However, many daughters speak about anger and violence in the home, which they found terrifying. Children who grow up in family systems where anger management is a problem, may not learn how to develop ways to stay or create inner calmness, as those around them are unable to teach them how to do this.

Some mothers grow up in a home with much anger, from both parents; maybe neither were violent, but it was very frightening for the child. Anger and domestic abuse usually take place behind closed doors and are kept as a family secret. In some families this is not possible, especially where families live in shared housing. Yet even if domestic abuse is overheard by neighbours, they will rarely act. I have heard many stories of people with responsibility in communities, such as the clergy and teachers, choosing 'not to see' what is in front of them, or of walking away from the evidence and abandoning a child to her fate. The shame that is carried by a child within an abusive system is heavy; they carry that shame to school and regularly lose sleep from their fears, and as a result may do less well in their studies. Shame is a painful feeling and often is not about anything that we have personally done, but what we have witnessed and what that says about our family and safety.

Shame is a painful feeling and often is not about anything that we have personally done

A daughter who might have experienced having something thrown at her, or who has been dragged by her hair or seen one parent attacking the other will carry these scars deep within her.

She was not protected by those who are supposed to protect her, either because her mother is the aggressor and there was no one to calm her or take her out of the situation, or the aggressor is another and the mother is frozen with fear. The cycle of domestic abuse is one that entraps both aggressor and victim. The abuse is usually followed a day later by pleading for forgiveness with promises that it won't happen again, and there is collusion in the hope that that will be the case; it rarely is. The little girl becomes numb so that she doesn't knowingly feel the terror, although her body systems do. She is caught in this cycle, with nowhere to go. She does what she can to survive physically and emotionally. Issues about safety and trust can become lasting legacies for both mother and daughter, and they are locked together in the memory of this violence.

Families can also be a forum where sexual abuse is perpetrated; where those we look to for protection and who are supposed to love us, do the opposite. This is such a shock and violation of our boundaries and brings deep shame. The dynamics of abuse by a family member or a respected member of the close community can compound the impact of abuse for the child. Think of the daughter who was sexually abused by an uncle, her mother's brother. He is likely to have told the child something like, "*This is special to the two of us and no one else must know. You mustn't tell your mother or there will be trouble.*" The abuser deliberately cuts out the mother from being able to support the child. The daughter may also fear telling her mother in case she is not believed, which unfortunately can sometimes be the case. She might fear telling her as she doesn't want to distress her, so protects the mother from reality. It might be that she wonders if her mother knows anyway and has abandoned her to it, and so the daughter suffers on her own. The difference between feeling believed or not, of feeling able to tell or not, is huge. Often the daughter becomes confused, as love and abuse merge in her mind, and she may take responsibility for the abuse, as in some way, that feels safer than accepting that someone who was supposed to protect her didn't. The abused child is unable to find a safe haven, anywhere.

We know that sexual harassment and abuse are not confined to families. The nature of the experiences we had and how they were dealt with, affects how safe we feel in the world and thus our behaviour. If these experiences happen in childhood and adolescence and we can talk to our mother about it, if we can get help and reassurance, then the impact is lessened. Where that doesn't happen, the impact will be unresolved, unconsciously affecting our behaviour and belief systems.

The cycle of domestic abuse is one that entraps both aggressor and victim

Being able to see the systemic dynamics behind any emotional challenges we have helps us step away from self-blame and see how we were all caught in the family system. Recognising the roles we might have been assigned or have taken on out of conscious awareness, and the levels of the emotional thermostat, brings a degree of awareness to us as we explore ourselves and our adult relationship with our mother. It has enabled me to see a different perspective of myself that I have found very valuable. These kinds of revelation may come about early or later in life – whenever we are ready for them.

There is a tendency to think that only those who have been affected by domestic or sexual abuse or abandonment carry emotional trauma. This is not the case. A lack of safety and unconditional love brings emotional trauma, as does not being wanted or being separated from our mother. It also results from life experiences as infants and children. As I have previously said, it is part of the human condition.

Spiral of Learning

Take some time to reflect on your family system and how you experienced it as a child. It is important only to reflect on these if it feels the right time for you to do so. For some, the emotional pain may still be so great that reflecting deeper alone and not in a therapeutic setting may not be helpful right now. Be mindful about what is healing for you. You can always return to reflect on these issues at another time. If it does feel okay to engage in this way, just let the responses arise within you. There are no 'right' answers. You may want to come back to the questions several times, and on each occasion you may get an additional response. You don't need to DO anything about your reflections, just let them sit in your awareness. You may find it helpful to write down your responses.

- *What words would you use to describe your family and how it operated?*
- *Did you pick up, or were given a particular role (mother's little helper, daddy's girl, the favourite, etc)? Might you still be carrying elements of that?*
- *What level was the emotional thermostat and how did that affect you then and now?*
- *What impact did and does the family dynamic have on your relationship with your mother?*

CHAPTER 4
Separation, Illness and Grief in Childhood Leave a Legacy

There are myriad significant experiences we have as children and adolescents that shape us and add to the nature of our emotional bond with our mother. These include illness, separation, grief, divorce, our schooling, having to move a lot or the family living in precarious situations due to racism, poverty, or imprisonment of a parent. Some children grow up in a war zone and with the terror of trying to leave it; the level of stress in some families can be high and debilitating. Whatever we experience will leave an emotional legacy within us.

Imagine a scenario in which a young daughter is ill. How her mother responds to her makes a big difference to the emotional legacy of that experience, together with how the family system handles illness and crises. Judith was diagnosed with a benign brain tumour as a child, the surgery was potentially life threatening and frightening for both Judith and her mother. Judith recalls thinking that she must do all she could to stop her mother feeling anxious about her health, and she has taken that coping mechanism into adulthood, still shielding her mother from any health concerns she may experience. Kate's mother responded differently to her childhood illness, which involved her being in bed and physically weak for some time. Her mother's anxiety took the form of smothering Kate's freedom and exploration of independence, even long after the illness had gone. In other instances, mothers may have not paid much attention to the needs of their daughters, being more interested in the impact on themselves. They later saying something like, *"You stopped me living my life for that year, it was so hard for me."* There are also mothers who are able to bring calm reassurance and a loving presence to such situations, often helped by having a supportive extended family around them.

Being hospitalised as an infant or child is a highly stressful and frightening experience due to the separation from our mother and our home. This can be softened by the hospital care given and by how the mother/parents are able to respond. When I started my career in nursing, a long time ago, parents were not allowed to stay in hospital with their children, nor visit outside strict visiting hours. Some children with tuberculosis were sent to sanitoriums for a year or more with very few visits from parents, often because the distances involved were too great. It was thought that children were distressed by parents visiting and then leaving, so it was deemed best to see the parents hardly at all. Once the child left hospital, things were miraculously expected to return to 'normal', as if such an extended separation had no impact on family systems. Fortunately, we now know how greatly this impacts a child's emotional life, and a parent staying with a young child is now the expectation but not always possible. However, depending on our age many of us might have experienced that total separation. We might not always make the link between our relationship in the present with our mother and these earlier experiences, but the increasing understanding about the impact of emotional experience is highlighting what these links may be.

Like some other daughters, Gill went to boarding school at eleven years old. The rationale often used by parents is that it is a way of providing stability for their child, preventing them from having to move schools every few years. Even though the motivation for the decision to do this might be caring, many children suffer from this kind of separation and from the educational institution which becomes their term-time surrogate family. Some children enjoy their boarding school experience making lasting friendships; others suffer it, often in silence, and are scared by it. Whatever other impacts children experience from this kind of separation, it undoubtedly has an effect on the relationship with their mother. This can be enhanced if a mother is indifferent to a daughter's distress and unhappiness.

Death of a parent

The death of a parent when we are young is a devastating loss. Not only is the child left bereft, but so is the other parent and any siblings. The whole family system is in shock and grief. My father died suddenly and unexpectedly when I was nine-years old, he was only 40. My four grandparents had died (suddenly, it seemed to me) in the preceding three - four years and these deaths occurring so quickly, one after another, was already emotionally difficult. My mother was left quite isolated, with little support around her. I was terrified about what would happen to me, as it never crossed my mind that my mother would be able to support us financially, because at that time in my type of family system, the father's salary was the primary source of income. I thought I would have to go to a children's home. This was my grieving imagination at work as there was no likelihood of this at all, and she was very capable of supporting us. However, with hindsight, I can see that whilst she could support us financially, she was less able to support her grieving children emotionally, as she had her own grief and the consequences of the death to manage. My family system knew a lot of grief and had, I think, become emotionally numbed by it. Mourning was not enabled or seen as important, the task being to 'get on with things.'

Many daughters suffer the death of a parent and the nature of the family system can support or inhibit the grief and fear a child feels. Children are often terrified of what will become of them. If their mother has died, an eldest child may feel they have to step in, however young, and take charge of the family and her siblings. This may also be a response to seeing a father unable to cope with the grief, further adding to the daughter's fear for her and her siblings' survival. Such daughters grow up very quickly; in that moment, the childhood ends. Many such daughters take a sense of responsibility into their adult life.

When one parent dies, a child often loses the other one to their grief

The extent to which we are helped, as children, to grieve depends on the culture of the society and family, and the ability of those around us to support us. Many of us may have been abandoned to our grief and in response we possibly numbed ourselves. Now,

51

there is much more awareness of the need to support bereaved children, to help them process their grief, and schools are so much better prepared. However, the family system needs to be open to help from outside, and it is a lot to ask of a grieving parent to manage their own grief and the practical implications of life, as well as to be sensitive to the differing needs of their children.

Divorce

The impact of divorce on children is well documented, they can get lost in the divorce process or used in a battle between the parents. Children usually but not always stay with their mother, who is likely to be stressed by the change in her circumstances, even if it is her choice. And, as I have said before, a stressed parent is stressful for a child. Consequent relationships with any step-parent can be happy and safe or unhappy and insecure. Each one will be on a continuum between these two poles. Whether the relationship is full or part-time, and whether the 'lost' parent is still alive and in contact or not, will all affect a child's emotional health. Having a new step-father who is aggressive or dismissive is hard enough to experience, but it is emotionally more affecting if our mother doesn't protect us from this behaviour, or when she chooses to stay with him rather than to protect us. Of course, it is understandable why some women make this choice: maybe they are afraid of financial insecurity; perhaps their own history means they cling to those who show them any crumb of attention; or they are afraid of the consequences of leaving and any harm that might ensue. Nonetheless, the impact on the child is lasting and deep, as it is with a step-mother who is hostile towards us and our father doesn't intervene.

The origin of the term 'step-mother' is that she 'steps into' the space left by the mother, which in previous generations would typically be through death. How she embraces the relationship with her step-daughter will depend on her history, her emotional security and her capacity to accept the child of her partner's previous relationship, and even that he/she had a previous relationship at all. Step-mothers in fairy tales are often portrayed as villains – one only needs to think of *Cinderella* or *Hansel and Gretel* – however, in the origins of many of these stories, it was the birth mother. not a step-mother who perpetrated the ill-deeds upon her daughter. Over the centuries, these stories were changed to protect the myth of the mother and to project the cruelty as coming from the step-mother. Some step-mothers and fathers are loving, welcoming and generous hearted to their step-daughter. Others however are not, they do not want the children in the new family nor do they want to acknowledge the existence of the mother. Daughters may connect well with the step-mother or may feel that rejecting her and blocking her influence is a way to protect the mother's legacy.

I have outlined a few of the more common life events that may have impacted us, but of course there are any number of situations that may affect us as babies and children, and consequently, into adulthood. In some ways I was fortunate as I had only a few – others have many more life events to contend with. Some daughters are required to take on a care-taker role of a chronically sick mother, or one with disabilities, from a very early age. The demands on them are great and it is almost impossible to continue with a childhood with little free time to play and develop their own live. They may miss some of their schooling or find it hard to study. They do an amazing job in caring in this way and some pay a high price in terms of the impact on them.

For others, life events involve moving house a lot, constantly changing schools and breaking up friendships; or a mother needing hospitalisation for physical or mental health reasons and the daughter being cared for by others, unable to visit her mother for months on end or not being told what was happening. Some children lose their close friends too. Wendy had two friends who died when she was around eight years old, one from polio and the other from a tragic freak accident. This will rock the emotional security of any child. Many of us will experience something similar when a beloved pet dies, or in some cases is removed without warning by a parent. At an early age, this loss can be huge because a pet is like a family member to a child, who is likely to have had a close attachment with the animal, feeling loved by it perhaps at a time she didn't feel loved by her parents. How these losses are handled enables grief to be fully expressed or restricts it, and either develops an already loving relationship with the mother/parent or puts another knot in the tangled web.

Whilst we can't change our history, we can change how it continues to impact us and our behaviour

The examples I have given so far are of things that are out of our influence; that happen to us. There may also be events where we were cruel to others – perhaps we were a bully at school or to our siblings or caused harm to others intentionally. I am talking here of serious events, not the run of the mill 'social learning' we all do – events that maybe haunt us and for which we carry guilt, so much so that we have never told anyone about it. If our family system was unloving or contained aggression or violence or we were abused, we might have acted that out on others as a way of trying to regain a sense of power instead of feeling helpless. Some daughters who are distressed by the relationship with their mother or parents may attempt to kill themselves and/or be offered therapeutic help.

No child grows up without life events or disturbances in their family systems. It is the intensity of the events and how the emotional impact on us is supported and processed that means the experience leaves lasting emotional markers within us, or not. Life events can get stuck and entangled within our web of experience and continue to affect us consciously and unconsciously as adults, in relation to ourselves, our mother and others. Whilst we can't change our history, we can change how it continues to act impact us and our behaviour, if we want to.

Spiral of Learning

The intention of reflecting on our own life experiences is to honour ourselves, not to become overwhelmed by emotions that may arise and then focusing on them. If we carry such emotions, then we may find a therapeutic process helpful, so that we are able to accept our reality without emotional pain or repeating old patterns. If it doesn't feel a good time for you to go through these suggestions, leave them and come back to them when it does. Looking after yourself is a sign of honouring yourself. If it feels right, you may find it helpful to write out your responses to these questions.

- *If you had to pick out three scenes from your early life, which stand out for you (positive as well as challenging), what would they be?*

  How have they affected you?

  What were the settings?

  Who was there?

  What was the impact on you?

- *How might any of the above affected your relationship with your mother as a child and now as an adult?*

- *In what ways may they still influence you in the present?*

CHAPTER 5
How We Develop Ideas about Ourselves

We develop ideas and beliefs about ourselves based on how those closest to us respond to us as infants and children. If our early relationships were not loving, safe and emotionally holding, it is likely to have been harder for us to develop a sense of our own individuality and talents. Our brain develops in correlation with our early relationships, and neural pathways are laid down that are consequently always 'switched on'. As a result, we grow up defining ourselves in great part by how others have treated us, although we can change these patterns if we want to, and many people do with therapeutic help or through self-awareness and enquiry. This is an ongoing process throughout our lives, as the grooves of our early experiences run deeply within.

These ideas about ourselves start with how we were looked at, talked to, touched and held, comforted and reassured, encouraged, and protected. We are highly sensitised to these interactions. We know in our gut if we aren't really wanted or loved for ourselves; we recognise the lie when behaviour and eyes betray something different. We can also grow up thinking we are wrong, that our gut sense isn't the 'truth'. We can get confused by the difference between what is said and what is enacted and lose trust in our own experience.

In observing mothers and children, we often see some touching and sensitive contact, but we may also see children in distress or fearful, whose feelings are dismissed or even punished. If our feelings are not validated or if expressing an emotion is punished, we grow up confused about what it is we experienced. Many daughters become confused about why they feel anger; they tell themselves it is wrong to feel angry and they shouldn't do it. It is likely that in their family system, anger wasn't allowed to be expressed, or if it was, it came out as violence. As a consequence, we don't learn about healthy anger, and we can become fearful of the emotion.

If we experienced a loving mother and family with good contact, in a system that supported emotional processing and encouragement for our growing selves, we have probably grown into women who are able to love and trust ourselves. Such women are more likely to be self-confident, able to believe in themselves and their capabilities, and have been able to develop their talents and skills in directions that bring them satisfaction and joy. That doesn't mean that such women don't have self-doubt or lose confidence, but that they are able to love themselves and have people around them who also love and encourage them. Such daughters are less likely to make life decisions that bring harm to them, or if they do, they remedy that situation rapidly.

If our early experience was more inclined to the shadow side of mothering and parenting – that is, where the loving contact was missing, unpredictable or variable—we may develop a belief that this is our fault, that we are somehow responsible. How could we think otherwise if we believe the myth that all mothers unconditionally love their children? As children, we are too emotionally immature to comprehend the impact of life events on our parents and what they are having to deal with. We respond to what is in front of us and to our physiological and emotional reactions. If we grew up being criticised or in a system that punished 'misbehaviour', we develop our own inner critic, our own inner negative voice which continues to berate us for 'getting things wrong' or 'being stupid' or 'not doing something perfectly'. Such daughters will often use negative self-talk or feel bad about themselves or punish themselves in a range of subtle ways.

We all respond to how we are mothered in our own ways, however, there are patterns. For example, feeling responsible for our mother's happiness is one. Another is the tendency to push ourself to be a high achiever, in whatever field, from a deep belief that says, *"then I will be loved"*. We might have developed determination to be successful in our chosen field, as a way to block out more difficult feelings that we are unable to process; this success brings with it many 'distractions' and is another way of trying to prove ourselves. We can also use busyness as a shield from our mother, as in "I am too busy next week to call in and see you." Rather than deal with the underlying issues in the relationship, we excuse ourselves by being busy.

Many of us internalised the voices of blame, dissatisfaction and judgement from our childhood as our own thoughts. We constructed self-critical beliefs as a way of trying to understand our situation as children. These can continue to bring us much suffering in adulthood. We may have learnt to hide parts of ourselves that were not welcomed or acknowledged, and we continue to fear they still may not be. Maybe we were a chatty, extrovert daughter, with a mother who wasn't and who found it frustrating to always have this child talking to her. She may well have given the impression that this part of our behaviour was not welcome, not natural even, leaving us feeling guilty or ashamed for 'talking too much' and thereby limiting our own enjoyment in life. Maybe we were bright and intelligent, more so than our mother, and she found that difficult to cope with and so she didn't encourage our learning and interests, or perhaps she warned us not to out-shine a sibling. We may have grown up believing our intelligence wasn't welcome in the world or struggled to find acceptable ways to express it. As adults, it doesn't help us when reflecting on such family dynamics, to point the finger of blame or try to 'get rid of' these beliefs and behaviours. Instead, we need to practise compassion for ourselves, and to be curious about why we developed these coping mechanisms in the first place and why we hold onto them now.

All our beliefs and thoughts about ourselves enabled us to adapt to our family circumstances; we developed our unique response to family life as a way of trying to understand our experiences so we could survive in the family system. Instinctively, we knew we had to become the child our mother/family system could cope with, and this was rooted in a deep fear of abandonment. This fear isn't necessarily a logical one but is a profoundly emotional one. Very rarely do families abandon their children, but it does happen, as the poet Lemn Sissay describes in his moving memoir, *My Name is Why*; his adoptive parents rejected him when he was around eleven, having treated him as a full member of the family. Laura Cumming describes in her book, *On Chapel Sands* how her mother was 'handed over', as a toddler, to another woman and was never told about it. It was kept a secret. Many of us will have read fairy tales where children were abandoned or punished for no good reason, and these can feed our fertile imagination, but fear of abandonment runs much deeper than stories; it is a primal fear. For our own survival we know we have to find a way to belong.

Abandonment can be hardwired into our evolutionary memory. It is highly likely that some of our ancestors will have lived in family circumstances – such as war, drought or famine – which led to children being passed on to others to be raised. Even the horror of infanticide may have been used to create a degree of stability in a family. As is the reality of infanticide, parents may kill a sickly child or leave them to die as a way of managing scarce resources of food and income. This occurs more often where women have no control over their fertility and where there is no state support for families. Infanticide may also be connected with mental ill health deterioration..

As adults, it doesn't help us when reflecting on family dynamics, to point the finger of blame. Instead, we need to practise compassion for ourselves, and to be curious about why we developed these coping mechanisms in the first place

With a loving, welcoming mother we don't need to repress emotional pain and anger, we don't need to go through contortions to adapt to her demand, we can freely discover ourselves with her. However, where the mother is not able to be loving and welcoming enough of the time, we have to do our best to adapt to her, and we may have to contort ourselves, rather like getting used to wearing an ill-fitting garment. We can get so used to being pulled out of our shape in this way that it feels normal, or at least very recognisable. The habit becomes so ingrained that the idea of taking off the metaphorical garment and freeing ourselves from the discomfort it brings can feel frightening. Not only might we risk a negative response from our actual mother, we might experience it from our own internalised mother-critic or that part of us that is scared of becoming more of ourselves.

If we have become so used to adapting to the needs of our mother, rather than prioritising our own needs, we can take this pattern of behaviour into our relationships with other people, both personally and at work. Other people may stimulate the same issues within us, for example, of not wanting to get things wrong, of wanting to rescue someone, of clinging-on out of fear of being abandoned, or of always feeling responsible for everything that happens. From our earliest relationships we learnt either that it is safe to be in close contact with others or that we should withhold our trust and be on our guard; we have learnt to trust others or to hold a level of mistrust. We all take what we learnt in the 'there and then' of our childhood into our relationships in the 'here and now' and we do it to protect our hurt inner child.

We can get so used to being pulled out of our shape that it feels normal, or at least recognisable

We can catch ourselves in patterns of thinking and behaving which while necessary as a child, no longer are in adulthood and have become habits that 'just happen' often without our noticing. We might say, *"That's just how I am"*. But what if we allow for the possibility that maybe that isn't just how we are and question whether we want to continue with that pattern? We can give ourselves the opportunity to notice thoughts and behavioural responses and habits and decide if they are bringing healthy outcomes for us. The old patterns can leave us feeling as if we are living someone else's life, and in some way we are, as we are only partly living our life while the other part is busy trying to please or protect ourselves from our mother.

We can give ourselves the opportunity to notice thoughts and behavioural responses and habits and decide if they are bringing healthy outcomes for us

If we are caught in a tangled relationship web with our mother, it is likely to feel difficult and challenging. These webs are intricately woven with many knots and repeating patterns and are unique to each family. The web can feel suffocating to our individuality and indeed parts of us are being numbed and abandoned in our effort to stay connected. At the heart of the difficult relationship with our mother is something about the life and death of us as separate individuals. Perhaps the most fundamental question we can ask of ourselves is, *"Can I live my own life, to my own inner rhythm or do I have to give up on that to be the daughter my mother demands of me?"*

Our Mother's Experience

It is important to recognise that everything I have written so far about the experience of daughters, could also have been our mother's experience as a daughter, explaining how she developed her unique sense of self; how she came to be who she is. She brings all her experience of being a mother from her mother, who brings hers from her mother and so on down the generations, all shaped by family context, life experience and the impact of the communities these women were born into and grew up in. The Russian Doll analogy helps us to see how interconnected we all truly are. If our mother had a loving upbringing, where she was helped to process the life events she experienced, she is more likely to choose a loving partner for herself, because she will honour herself in that way. If she didn't and hasn't been able to free herself as an adult from behaviour patterns she witnessed and internalised, she will be entangled in a more sticky and binding web of relationships. As a result, she might choose a partner(s) who isn't caring and loving, who may not treat her honourably, and to whom she might either cling or repeatedly leave.

What do you know about your mother's experience as a daughter? And of your grandmother's experience? We may know a lot or much has been hidden from us. I learnt quite a bit about my mother's and grand-mother's childhood from her, and now I have her short memoire that tells me more. It enabled me to understand what both she and my grandmother had had to endure and survive, and gave me insights into our relationship and why our family system was as she created it.

What do you know about your mother's experience as a daughter? And of your grandmother's experience as a daughter?

As well as our mother, and those closest to us within the family, other factors affect our sense of identity. The colour of my skin and my heritage were never factors in doors being closed to me, nor to feeling my difference at every turn. I only know second-hand the toxic impact of racism on a young child and her family. Many women have written of this experience, and I am grateful that they have done so. When I think of my childhood, a long time ago, all the books I read and the TV programmes I watched, had predominantly white characters, and those who were not, were rarely positively presented. I was fed reinforcing images and ideas about myself that I could identify with. What if I had been a child with parents of different ethnic heritage, or I was different from the majority in my class at school? I would have learnt early on, depending on when and where I was born, that there was no one (or only outcasts) who looked like me. I might have also learnt that something about me wasn't welcomed or liked, as I would have sensed or known that I was treated differently; and maybe I only came across few positive role-models. Family systems such as these will have known how this felt for generations and will have created ways of defending and protecting themselves against it. Societal racism is deeply toxic and family systems do their best to survive it. This affects how daughters come to see themselves as reflected by society, and they may internalise those beliefs and thoughts.

A daughter's skin colour may also be different from that of

her father or mother, or from either if adopted. If her skin colour differs from her mother, on whom she depends for so much in relation to growing her own sense of herself and her identity, her mother may engage with this in a deep and meaningful way recognising that race is an issue for her daughter. The mother may stand up against her extended family if they express racist views and take the risk of being abandoned by the family system as her daughter's needs feel more important. Some mothers who may find it hard to connect with their daughter may deny there is an issue to engage with at all, as they have never experienced it for themselves and are frightened of what it might mean. A daughter needs to find a way of navigating this complexity of projections from society, what she might absorb from her family (positive or not) and what she knows about herself from the inside. Her mother may be her strongest ally in this or inhibit it.

If we were born with female sexual characteristics, were raised as a girl and identify as one, our first point of learning about being a woman is from our mothers (and aunts) as our primary role-models. This might mean we adopt similar thoughts of what it is to be a woman, which may be positive or not, or we reject her model outright and find our own. We are also shaped by the demands and expectations of the society we live in, about what being a woman should or must mean. Transwomen who now identify as daughters, and transmen who now identify as sons face other challenges within society and maybe their families. Many of us were raised in a male-dominated culture and that impacts greatly on women in general, and on mother and daughter roles. Gender politics has changed greatly since I first became engaged with the feminist thinking and action in the 1960s/70s in the UK.

And, at the same time, a lot hasn't changed. We can be 'trained' to put males first, to go along with what they say or want; to believe certain occupations and roles are 'not for us' and to find that education process doesn't really include us. We can also learn that we 'should' keep quiet. Many of us have rejected these but may occasionally get caught out, or some are so subtle we don't recognise how they still influence us.

Whatever societal pressures on us as daughters and mothers can also limit how we see and think about ourselves. For example, it is not uncommon for the daughter to be expected to be the main care giver to an elderly parent, rather than a son. Sometimes, the expectation is that the unmarried or childless daughter will pick up this role rather than the married sister with children.

How we are enabled to develop into ourselves fully, and process our emotional experience, can be facilitated well by our mother and those around us or made harder for us

Spiral of Learning

These questions come at influences on us as children in a slightly different way:

- *Who did you admire when you were young, real or fictional, human, animal or fantasy character (exclude parents and siblings). What was it that you admired?*
- *What's your favourite story from fiction (film, book, TV) or one that was told to you over and over? What's its appeal for you?*
- *What mottos or sayings did you hear repeatedly in your family? What has their impact been on you?*
- *If you had to make a newspaper headline that captured all this what would it be?*
- *What links, if any, do you make with how you are today?*

PART 2

WHAT'S GOING ON NOW AND WHY?

Personal Reflection (2)

Today is my wedding anniversary. My oft-told story about my mother's part in my wedding has always been that she didn't support it or me, and that whilst she briefly turned up, she didn't stay and didn't involve herself in the planning. I have repeatedly been hurt by my version of the situation for 39 years. Today I had a different thought – that I had deliberately pushed her away as I feared her disapproval or 'interference' in ways I imagined I didn't want. I had created this drama and deepened my suffering. My actual pain was because we weren't emotionally close at the time, and for all I know, that might have been painful for her, too. If I had thought about it, I'd have known she'd have no idea what was expected of her by me, but I had never talked to her about it nor involved her in my planning of it. I now realise I could have talked with her about it all whilst still maintaining how I wanted it to be. I didn't have to block her out, and whilst involving her might not have worked out well, I didn't give it a chance. Alternatively, I could have blocked her out but then not blamed her for the consequences. But I didn't know then what I know now, and I didn't have the skills then that sometimes I can draw on now.

I realised as I redrafted this book, that I had become overtaken by a 'wounded child' archetype within me. I was only talking to and from that place – from the perspective of the wounded child – and I was always incredulous when daughters were surprised that such difficult relationships exist. It was good to be reminded of this, as it was an opportunity to reflect on what was going on within me.

Perhaps my envy blinded me? Perhaps I was stuck in my narcissistic (self-interested) drama rather than dealing with the full scope of reality?

CHAPTER 6

How the Past, the 'There and Then', Operates in the Present, the 'Here and Now'

We have all probably had an experience of family gatherings, where old behaviour patterns replay and sibling rivalry comes to the fore, and it is as if we are transported back into our childhood homes. Some of our interactions as an adult with our mother may also have that familiar feeling of repeating old patterns of behaviour. Unresolved experiences from the 'there and then' of childhood continue to reverberate and repeat in the 'here and now' of adulthood. This doesn't have to be the case, and change is possible, but things won't change unless there is an awareness and understanding of the relationship dynamics at play and our habitual thoughts that go with them.

As I set out previously, we are all on a Continuum of Closeness in our relationship with our mother, which might have changed over time. If we are at the loving, kindly, warm, supporting and encouraging end of the spectrum, it is likely that the relationship feels appropriately boundaried and neither woman is merged with the other. For example, our mother doesn't treat us as an extension of herself and we don't identify with her or her suffering. Neither takes control of the other's life nor feels a victim to the other and there is no power play going on. There may be disagreements of course, and perhaps some personality differences show themselves at times, but these can be over-looked, or talked about and resolved without accusation. If you have had and continue to have a relationship with her like this, you are likely to have replicated elements of it in your relationships with others.

Some daughters enjoy being with their mothers and may say: *"She is an amazing woman, often giving me wise counsel and is always there as support. I don't feel I* **have** *to phone or see her, but I want to when it fits in with my life, which is quite often. She is good fun and when as a child I would have friends around, she welcomed them all"*. Within these types of relationships there is give and take; it doesn't mean that neither can be a bit sharp with each other at times, but there is a mutual respect and trust in each other.

Such relationships have little of the shadow side operating from the mothers, or from the daughter – by which I mean no hidden agendas, no competitive jealousy, or habitually vindictive behaviour. The foundations for trust and companionship have blossomed into this adult relationship, held together by their flexible web of connection. Some of us who have not experienced this type of relationship and are on a different point of the continuum may not have any sense of what a healthy relationship might be like in practice.

Even loving and holding relationships will have tensions at

times, and there can be occasional personality clashes. It is un-realistic to expect our relationships always to be plain sailing, and part of the skill of those in a loving relationship is negotiating these blips, and not taking them personally, of being able to talk through anything that arises that might have felt difficult. Daugh-ters who experience the relationship like this may say *"I do feel loved by Mum, and I hope she feels loved by me. At times, it's if some strange energy has entered into our connection, as if we want something from each other that we can't give. Then it goes away. We do sometimes talk about it afterwards, and neither of us holds a grudge about it."*

Maybe you are towards the other end of the continuum and experience your relationship with your mother as difficult, chal-lenging, hurtful and demanding? You may feel responsible for your mother, dutiful towards her, wanting to protect or rescue her. You may also feel anger and rage which is 'swallowed down' and repressed or hard to control. Such relationships have evolved from our attempts to get the contact, love, attention and interest in us that we may not have felt as children. It is also common that we take these ways of relating into other relationships. For example, if we have taken on the role of rescuer in relation to our mother, we are likely to rescue others as one of our core ways of relating.

Along the continuum are combinations of emotions and cir-cumstances, sometimes loving and supporting and at other times distressing and hurtful. The majority of daughters will probably experience a mix of these, but for others who find themselves in the shadows, their experiences will likely be mostly hurtful. What changes along the continuum is the energy that predominates most of the time. In shadow times we try to get our unmet emotional needs from the 'there and then' fulfilled in the 'here and now' or use our defences to protect ourselves from further hurt.

In turning our attention to the present relationship with our mother, it helps to be aware of some of the factors that have influenced it, so that we can break through denial and illusion. Where the relationship is difficult, we are locked in a pattern of relating and have both taken up roles within that. The daughter who is a 'rescuer' or 'protector' may be entangled with a 'helpless' mother or a 'child-mother' – one who doesn't take responsibility for herself as if she has not fully come into her adulthood. A daughter who is a 'controller' may have grown up in a chaotic family, or with a mother who through mental illness or addiction wasn't able to offer structure to the child. An 'exasperated hurt' daughter may be caught up with a 'self-interested' mother, someone who is narcissistic and for whom nothing is enough. A hurt daughter may have a mother who criticises often and always has done. As we know, we can't change our mother, but we can become aware of the role we have taken up and the patterns we perpetuate whilst also looking into what really lies beneath them. We may find a fear of abandonment which takes us straight back to childhood. Duty may be replacing the repressed anger that has been repeatedly swallowed down. Everything we experience with our mother is a point of entry into raising our awareness of the unconscious motivations that underlie our behaviour.

Shifts happen in the relationship as our mother ages and her circumstances change; perhaps she is widowed or her partner leaves her later in life. Maybe the impact of some of her earlier life decisions are becoming more problematical. Many daughters with elderly mothers feel unable to do anything about the relationship, assuming any transformation isn't possible. They feel tied and then guilty for counting the years she remains alive and demanding of them; then they may hide the guilt by being reluctantly dutiful. However, the good news is that we can always reassess our part in the relationship and it is possible to find a way to be caring to a sick and ailing mother to whom we have not felt close to, loved or seen. We need to be clear about our boundaries and the choices we make, then take responsibility for them. Chapter 21 sets out to create a healthy care-taking relationship if that is what is wanted.

Everything we experience with our mother is a point of entry into raising our awareness of the unconscious motivations that lie behind our behaviour

Transforming the relationship in terms of moving from a difficult one to a loving holding one, is usually not possible. There is too much unresolved history between both parties, and often only one part of the relationship considers it to be a problem. That could be the mother of course, who doesn't know how to move beyond the patterns, especially if her daughter seems unaware of her desire for change. Such a mother might respond positively to the daughter changing her own patterns and the seeds of a refreshed relationship might be sown. However, for each of us our responsibility is to ourselves; we can only achieve happiness or contentedness if we make it happen for ourselves. If we want to have our needs met, we need to find a way to achieve this that isn't subversive or perpetuates past hurts. I learnt that many adults carry the magical thinking of a young child that says, *"If I take care of (rescue, protect, parent) my mother, my turn will come."* Of course, our turn never comes unless we take it for ourselves. Another magical thought that I identified with is, *"If only I try hard enough, I will be loved."* This also doesn't work, and eventually I realised I need to love myself.

While focusing on daughters' experiences of their relationship with their mothers, it can appear that it is the mother who is making life difficult, but it would be an illusion if we were to believe that it is only mothers who are the problem, or if we say, *"It isn't us it is her"* without fully examining our part in it. In so doing, a daughter may come to realise she is 'clinging on' to her mother, not taking responsibility for herself and continuing to want her mother to be the grown up. This might not even be experienced as a difficult or challenging relationship, as long as the mother is willing to play the game and has a vested interest in keeping her daughter in the 'child' role. It may only be experienced as difficult if the mother refuses to do this and the daughter keeps up the game and gets rebuffed. If this has some resonance for us, we need to look more deeply into the dynamics we have set up.

Some daughters behave in ways that are narcissistic, entitled, controlling, hurtful or demanding in relation to their mother. We too, can be negative and critical, passively or overtly aggressive. Some daughters may have mental health problems which can lead to erratic or attacking behaviour. Mothers respond to such behaviour in different ways maybe rescuing, protecting or being dutiful, and are caught in the entanglement. Raising our awareness means looking closely at our own shadow sides and what deeper feelings hold the patterns in place. We tend to see all our patterns as honourable, but we need to be very honest with ourselves. This is not about blaming ourselves but taking responsibility as a healthy adult for our behaviour.

In recent years the prevalence of neuro-diversity is now recognised. Some forms of this may make emotional closeness and relationships challenging for the neuro-diverse person and those close to them. In retrospect, it is clear that some of our mothers may have been diagnosed as neuro-diverse. Similarly, mothers who suffered post-natal depression were not properly diagnosed but rather treated with impatience and a lack of understanding. Daughters too, may not be aware of their own neuro-diversity. I know of several people in their 60s and 70s who have only recently been diagnosed as neuro-diverse, and who welcomed that it made sense to them about things they had found difficult. Where this is present in mother or daughter, we need to draw on the current understanding that is now available and factor it into our reflections and thinking about change.

Raising our awareness means looking closely at our own shadow sides

In any relationship between a daughter and her mother there are two 'there and thens' at play – ours and hers. There are also different family systems: the one of our childhood that our mother may continue to enforce and the one we have created with our own family. We develop different allegiances with our partners who bring in their 'there and then' history. How our mother responds to our partner also becomes part of the mix. A mother may seem very put out that she is no longer the prime focus of her daughter's life anymore or might flirt with her daughter's partner. Mothers from the loving end of the continuum don't need to do this.

Entanglement is all about the 'there and then' operating in the 'here and now'

Spiral of Learning

As with all Spiral of Learning suggestions, if any of them feel too emotionally challenging right now, leave them, go and do something enlivening and resourcing for yourself. You can always return to them later if you want to.

You don't need to act on your responses to these reflective questions. It is enough to just bring them into your awareness. You may find it helpful use your Reflective Journal to capture your thoughts and feelings so that you can come back to them at a later stage.

- *What thoughts come immediately to you when you think of your 'there and then' operating in the 'here and now'? What behaviour responses, thoughts, self-beliefs or emotions may be from the past but operating in the present?*

- *It may be helpful for you to form these thoughts into a short story, which of course you can fictionalise to bring about the ending you desire. All forms of writing are an ordered way of bringing our thoughts into coherence and allow us to explore potentialities that we've never considered before. Be playful or courageous with your story, allow your creativity to flow.*

- *Alternatively, maybe you'd rather create an image(s), with coloured pencils or felt-tips, that captures the essence of your inner experience. As for the story, be playful and courageous. Enjoy the activity.*

CHAPTER 7

Difficult Adult Daughter: Mother Relationships and What Holds Them In Place

Difficult relationships take many forms, what they share is an absence of emotional connection and a desire to fill the void that creates. Whatever patterns have evolved, you could say that there is a kind of love in the interaction; there is a bond, at least, that comes from the lifetime of connection and a desire perhaps to express love. However, these patterns are of distorted love, and there will have been many causal factors for why they have evolved. The roots are likely to be from core fears of abandonment, of feeling unloved or unwanted and are ways of staying in relationship, however painful. They are formed by our attempts to stay close to mothers who may be emotionally unavailable, or critical, or are narcissistic or who may have a mental illness or addiction. The environment around us both in the past can also push us into a way of relating that is entangled.

There are many variations in fraught relationships between

daughters and their mothers, and each is unique to them both. There are also common patterns that can be identified to help us understand more about the patterns of behaving that keep us locked together. Trying to create a definitive list is an impossible task but I have described a few that appear to be most prevalent:

- Dutiful and resentful
- Rescuing, parenting or protecting
- Self-sacrificing
- Feeling responsible
- Feeling smothered
- Avoidance and distance
- Hurt and silent
- Angry and possibly hating

These are not mutually exclusive, and the emotions experienced may arise in any of the types of relationships. Many daughters feel hurt and remain silent, and angry or hating; they feel deep resentment from not being thanked, or acknowledged or respected as separate individuals, despite all they do. Another shared emotion is often an overwhelming sense of responsibility held by the daughter for the mother's wellbeing. We can also feel shame about how we feel towards our mother, hating her or wanting her to disappear from our lives. This shame may prevent us from talking personally about our experience.

What gets lost in entangled relationships is loving connection. Daughters can harden themselves to be able to stay connected, repressing their emotional hurt and needs while feeling ashamed about the anger and resentment they feel.

Dutiful and resentful

Many daughters describe themselves as dutiful and resentful. For some, it is a way of managing a relationship with a mother who is self-absorbed in that their needs trump everyone else's. We can feel our life and needs don't really exist in our mother's awareness. For others it is a way of managing our hurt and silence or anger. To try to bridge this gap in connection we 'do our duty', turning up, looking out for, and attending to, our mother. Often this feels onerous. Dutiful daughters to such mothers may talk of finding it hard to love their mother, of finding her demands burdensome and of feeling great resentment.

What is it to be dutiful? It is a sense of obligation, a responsibility or task that goes with a particular role. It isn't about personal emotional connection, or the meeting of mutual needs. Maybe we feel *'she raised me so now I have to attend to her'*. There is often an expectation that the unmarried daughter should assume this caretaking role, especially if she doesn't have children. Some mothers make this explicitly clear to their daughter, leaving no option for their daughter not to comply. The mother might see her daughter as an extension of herself, disregarding the fact that her daughter is a separate individual with her own life and pressures. Healthy relationships have equal amounts of give and take. Dutiful relationships are not reciprocal, energy runs only one way: toward the mother.

There is something else going on around the resentment. We can decide to be dutiful, or a protector or rescuer, to fill the gap if we want, but if that carries with it a hope that we will close the gap by doing that, we are setting ourselves up to suffer. If resentful daughters recognise that they carry this hope and can let it go, they no longer have to carry the resentment that burns inside.

Healthy relationships contain equal amounts of give and take. Dutiful relationships are not reciprocal

Rescuing, parenting or protecting

Many of us are caught up as rescuers, protectors, and parents to our mothers. We step in, becoming care-takers to our mothers, rescuing her from the impact of her life decisions, sorting out and arranging things for her. If our mother is upset, we jump into the role we have taken on as her practical helper. Despite our commitment to being active, loving daughters, we often end up feeling resentful and guilty for feeling resentful. We can also feel burdened by the demands we are expected to meet. An entangled care-taking role is one where we are seeking love and contact through our rescuing, parenting or protecting, we are trying to bridge the gap in closeness and hoping to get the attention back that we crave. We rarely get the acknowledgement or thanks we seek and feel resentful and burdened, and yet we continue with the pattern of relating that is unsatisfying. We may think *'my turn will come'* or that *'if I try hard enough, I will be acknowledged and valued, one day'*. Many of us have organisational skills which make us good practical helpers, however, it is the hope for emotional contact and the pattern of relating that makes us entangled.

Rescuing, like its cousins protecting and parenting, can be a subtle form of control. We are saying to ourselves that the person we rescue is unable to decide for themselves and so we become a heroic 'first responder' as if we were the saviour paramedic. It can be a defence against feeling helpless or frightened by a parent's inability to manage their life, both of which scenarios are terrifying to a small child. Every time we rescue, we are reinforcing the idea that this is our role in the other person's life. We may then feel burdened by the expectation that we will continue to do this. This is how we further entangle the web.

Becoming the parent to the mother often arises where a mother falls into a dependent role or is seen as unable to manage her own life or tells her daughter she can't. It could be that mother has an addiction or mental health problem who was, and remains, unable to manage her life herself. They have looked for a rescuer and found one. If a child has seen her mother being unable to manage her life, the anxiety provoked is likely to encourage the daughter to take on parenting as a way of managing that response.

Being a daughter of a mother who has a drink problem, for instance, is very challenging. Alcohol addiction, and some forms of mental illness, bring unpredictable and sometimes aggressive behaviour into the family, which would frighten a little girl. She may grow up wanting to control the chaos, so becomes a parent to the mother. Such relationships, as with a mother who is narcissistic, can be highly demanding and at times may make the daughter want to scream with frustration and experience hatred. Despite all that, a daughter may still blame herself and think *'if only I had been different'*. It can be a relief when the mother dies, although the daughter may feel shame and guilt with that relief.

Sometimes rescuing takes on a slightly different form, if a daughter and her mother were victims of domestic abuse. Protection can become a key function within a relationship where both mother and daughter were witness to, or subject to, physical violence. Seeing a mother's vulnerability and fear would be very distressing to a daughter who was helpless to stop the violence, and she may grow up feeling she failed her mother. The daughter might have been trained from an early age by her mother to take on a protector role which she stays in, continuing to feel guilty perhaps that she can't protect her mother from the past. In response, and from feeling compassion for her mother, she may continue to want to make her mother's life alright.

It is not surprising that protection is such a key issue in their relationship and others like it. The violence and the fear that they experienced was never discussed, but it is always there in the background. It is not the child's responsibility to protect the mother although the child will have felt powerless and at times terrified when witnessing the dynamics in the household. The mother will also carry many conflicting emotions about being unable to protect herself or her daughters. Often this kind of violence is hidden from others, and no one else witnesses what is happening. It is held between the mother and her children but cannot be aired perhaps because it might bring up too many difficult and conflicting feelings for all concerned, which would be emotionally challenging.

Some daughters may resist doing their own therapeutic work about the impact of the violence on them out of a sense of duty to their mothers or as another form of protecting them from the reality of what they both experienced. As a result, the old patterns and their impact on the daughter remain in place.

Rescuing, like its cousins protecting and parenting, can be a subtle form of control

Self-sacrificing

This is another form of rescuing. It may involve holding ourselves back so as not to out-shine our mother or ignoring our own needs in order to be of service to her. A mother may be envious of her daughter's looks or intelligence or opportunities, and subtly or directly undermine her daughter's achievements. Our mother may appear to want us to sacrifice our life and relationships in service to her. We may try to protect our mother from feeling regrets about her life choices or protect her from her own sense of failure or disappointment. If so, we carry a belief that our mother couldn't cope with these feelings.

This self-sacrificing behaviour occurs within daughters who give of themselves for the betterment of their mother, regardless of the consequences for them. The daughter may believe they must do this for the sake of their mother. Such daughters may find it hard to acknowledge their own disappointment in their mothers. As for all entangled relationships, these patterns of relating can be exhausting and diminishing, and the impact on us often is emotionally intense. Our frustration, resentment, hurt from not being acknowledged, anger and possibly hatred are sometimes hard to experience and acknowledge.

The Responsible Daughter

One of the features of entangled relationships is that of feeling responsible for the other person. This keeps us rescuing, being dutiful, parenting, protecting and self-sacrificing.

Those who carry a huge sense of responsibility for their mother's wellbeing are likely to carry that into other areas of their life. We can feel responsible for many things though we are not and put a lot of energy into trying to sort things out.

An over-riding sense of responsibility may develop in relation to mothers who appear unable or unwilling to take responsibility for their own lives, for whatever underlying reason. Such a daughter may carry a fear of what will become of her mother without this support, and perhaps feels that she couldn't bear the feeling of letting her down. It can also be an attempt to express compassion for our mother's approach to life but often at considerable cost to ourselves.

Why might a daughter feel she has to take on responsibility for her mother, when her mother doesn't do that for herself? To understand that we need to go back in time. It is likely that the mother has never really taken responsibility for her actions and the young daughter will have seen that. This may have left a daughter feeling unsafe and scared, leading to a determination to be responsible for her mother in small ways. Maybe her mother never really bonded or connected with her emotionally, so the daughter develops this way of relating hoping to get love and be noticed, to demonstrate a value when she doesn't feel valued. Many daughters illustrate clearly how the pattern they have evolved in relating to their mothers can so easily become a pattern for relating to others. They may say: *'I take responsibility for mother, so I take responsibility for others. I am a rescuer in all areas of my life. I self-sacrifice for mother, and I do the same for others. I feel protective of mother, and I feel protective of others.'*

Such patterns may be a way for a daughter to suppress her feelings of rage at her mother's inadequacy, which may have been there from childhood and never been resolved. There can be repercussions for a daughter who does this, as supressing one's true feelings for years can sometimes present as illness or disability, because these feelings are held in the body. The sharp end of a daughter taking on all the responsibility in the relationship is that she may eventually turn on her mother in anger. She may meet her desire to 'kill' the mother, not literally but emotionally.

As with all these relationships, it doesn't heal the emptiness that the daughter might feel at the absence of emotional connection. Meanwhile, the hope that it will continues and becomes a habitual way of relating.

Taking responsibility for another is a form of rescuing which is often present in more difficult mother/daughter relationships

The Smothered Daughter

In this example, the daughter is smothered by her mother's attention. Smothering mothers might look loving from the outside, in that they seem to like lots of contact and involvement, but from the daughter's perspective appearances are deceptive. This behaviour isn't loving, it is attention seeking. A smothering mother might be on the phone a lot of the time, maybe several times a day; she might try to push herself into the centre of the daughter's life offering help or support. The daughter can feel she has no space and finds it hard to block her mother's attention.

Some mothers see their daughter as an extension of themselves. We could see this as a mother who is very insecure in her lovability, which takes us back into her childhood. It could be that she never really developed into her own personhood because of her family context, and so she has no sense of herself as being a separate person, that is, an individual in her own right. In some ways she is more like a needy child. She has merged with her daughter as a way of filling the vacuum that resulted from her own childhood. This is another example of how love can become distorted.

Some maternal patterns are very persistent, they have been established over a lifetime. It can be hard to mark out clear boundaries, articulating them and repeatedly putting them in place, particularly with a mother we think we should respond to. Feeling bad is what stops us, and we needn't feel bad, it is a self-judgement and maybe one that was fed into us as children *'don't be horrid to mummy, she just wants to help you'*. We can feel compassion for her but it we don't have to rescue her. We can be kind and caring AND establish boundaries.

Some mothers see their daughter as an extension of themselves

Avoidance and Distance

This is a slightly different form of entanglement from those associated with care-taking. The entanglement shows itself by how we try to manage the relationship and the longing for, and hope that, we will get the love and attention we crave. Emotional distancing can take many forms. Some mothers, due to their history and circumstance, are not able to connect emotionally with their daughter so are emotionally distant. Others may have left the family system early on, maybe at the daughter's birth, or have put a physical distance between them and their daughter.

Our mother might never have been emotionally close, perhaps

we have felt little connection with her, and yet, we continue to hope that one day that will change. Some mothers didn't touch or cuddle their daughters, they may always have been experienced as cold and detached. As a daughter to such a mother, we may feel angry and frustrated, and hurt by the lack of attention and compassion we experience. If we say anything, almost pleading for a loving response, our mother may blame us for being too needy or sensitive and push us away and yet, we return again and again. As with all entangled relationships, we keep trying and keep suffering.

Alternatively, a daughter may deliberately put physical distance between her and her mother, finding too much contact painful. Using distance is a way we can protect ourselves, especially if we have reason to fear our mother or if contact with her is too upsetting for us. Distancing doesn't necessarily mean we are no longer entangled but have found a way to manage it for now. Our thoughts and emotions, including fear of being too near to our mother, keep us entangled and having to work hard to manage those emotions. While we carry these unprocessed emotions, we continue to carry the consequences of how we think about ourselves and possibly, how we relate to other people. Intimacy can come to raise deep fears that we will be hurt again. We may develop ways to keep others at a distance too.

Some mothers absented themselves from their daughter's lives through adoption or leaving the family. Daughters who are adopted may have a loving and close relationship with their adoptive mother. If they haven't, they may distance themselves or become entangled. How those who were adopted think about their birth mother varies considerably, some may not want a relationship at all, others may develop contact and have a satisfactory relationship as an adult, while some may become entangled through longing for emotional connection. For some daughters, the quest to find, be acknowledged and feel wanted by the 'lost mother' can be a driving force that takes them into entanglement.

Some 'lost mothers' respond positively to the contact, do not try to entrap their daughter, and negotiate what kind of relationship might be possible that would be mutually satisfying. It is where this isn't offered that the risk of entanglement arises. Daughters might have a story going in their head about how important it would be to have ongoing contact, even that which wasn't satisfactory. Where a 'lost mother' seeks to compromise or manipulate the relationship, the daughter may go along with it because of the hope she carries that it will 'fill the gap'. In so doing she may become a rescuer or be repeatedly hurt or take on a role. It can be hard to separate again and breaking off the connection can activate any underlying emotions of loss and abandonment. It is very distressing to be in a birth relationship with someone who has little capacity to see you for who you are, who creates distance between you and then acts as if it is your fault. You can 'hang on in there' hoping for something to resolve, but the repeated pattern of seeking closeness and getting none brings anger and suffering.

It is very distressing to be in a birth relationship with someone who has little capacity to see you for who you are, who creates distance between you and then acts as if it is your fault

The Hurt and Silent Daughter

All daughters who have suffered from the dark side of mothering feel hurt. We register emotional pain in the same parts of our brain as we do physical pain. It is as draining to feel emotional pain over years as it would be to have any chronic pain. A hurt daughter may have experienced criticism upon criticism about decisions she made, friends she had, what she wears, and how she lives. We may have developed a coping mechanism to laugh it off with her, while being overwhelmed by tears when we leave her. It can feel as if the mother is trying to 'kill off' aspects of the daughter and to take away pleasure the daughter may have in herself and her choices. The constant criticism of how we look, or the undermining of our decisions or 'tut tutting' about our plans is a form of sabotage. It plants the seeds of self-doubt which can sprout within us and take root, making us vulnerable to negative comments.

Perhaps the mother isn't critical, she just doesn't acknowledge anything her daughter achieves or does. A daughter can feel hurt from never feeling seen or supported or feeling loved. Hurt daughters often keep silent. They swallow down the tears and possibly anger. They don't say *'It really hurts me when you...'* We take on the pain, again as the price we think we have to pay to stay in connection.

A danger we need to look out for is living though a version of 'the wounded child' archetype. We may become so identified with it that it becomes the focus of our relationship, and we take pride in collecting evidence of how hurtful it is. It can become our narrative to which we keep adding, *'and another thing....'* While not really attending to ourselves and our wound, we have become the victim in the story and thus keep the focus on our mother. We stop thinking about what might work for us in this relationship, instead putting up defences and tests for her which she repeatedly fails, whilst perhaps giving no attention to the times when she might be loving.

By exploring my own responses as a daughter, I reflected on how my mother might have responded to her relationship to her mother. All entangled mothers carry their own pain and suffering, and how they act towards us are ways they try to manage their own inner turmoil. Critical mothers may have had critical mothers or carers. We take in critical mothering, parenting or schooling and it becomes internalised within us, part of how we relate to ourselves. We may criticise ourselves and be critical towards others. We can notice this and change our inner voice.

The danger for the hurt and silent daughter is that we can live our whole lives through this identity becoming so identified with it that we take pride in collecting evidence of how hurtful it is

The Hatred of the Angry Daughter
Just as the dark side of mothering creates emotional pain, it can also generate hatred and anger. That hatred might be for the mother or turned inwards towards ourselves. It can lead us to being cruel towards our mother or ourselves. Some daughters express their anger healthily but most of us are unable to do that. We may recognise that our anger slips out at times or that we are occasionally deliberately cruel to our mother in the words we use.

Mothers can blame us for *'not doing enough'* or *'not providing the right kind of help'* or questioning our motives or telling us we are uncaring. They may consistently ignore our needs and accomplishments, and may rarely, if ever, thank us for what we do for them. In the context of an entangled relationship these can generate anger and hatred within us. There can also be the anger from childhood experiences when we were physically or emotionally hurt or ignored or blamed for things we didn't do. The hatred and anger that we feel for the wounds inflicted upon us can often be overwhelming. Some daughters will act on this anger, which can have far-reaching consequences, others will suppress it, which can result in ill health.

Just as the dark side of mothering creates emotional pain, it can also generate hatred and anger. That hatred might be for the mother or turned inwards towards ourselves

The roles and relationships described above illustrate that in difficult relationships, the daughter takes up a role in response to the mother's behaviour, which often just exacerbates the situation. This behaviour is likely to have been acquired in childhood and may have become more pronounced with age or be one that is seemingly, demanded of us which we feel we have to take on. There are no healthy outcomes in these roles and the tangled web just becomes more tightly knotted over time. For many daughters there is self-recrimination and guilt while for others there is anger and distress. For all there is sheer exhaustion from the effort of trying to manage our relationship with our mother, to defend ourselves and 'be a good daughter'. Sometimes the feeling of hatred is so overwhelming that daughters need to dissociate entirely from the relationship. In doing so, they are set free but unless the feelings of hatred are relinquished or resolved, the hatred can become corrosive.

I repeat here that in any of these patterns of relating, the roles could be reversed. The mother may take on rescuing or protecting or feeling dutiful. She may feel smothered by her daughter or become self-sacrificing. The daughter may take up the 'helpless', dependent role despite being an adult. Maybe she has a chronic health condition, and the care-taking function has moved from being healthy to entangled. The mother is trying to bridge a gap in loving connection and may carry guilt that the daughter is as she is. We need to look closely at ourselves, and to whether any of this relates to us and our relationship with our mother.

What frees us ultimately, is attending to ourselves with compassion and without blame, looking deeply into our part in these relationships, of why we keep going back for more and how this brings us repeated suffering. Then, we can examine how we are weaving the web, and what we are able to do to disentangle ourselves from it.

Spiral of Learning

The suggestions below are designed to help you reflect and learn from the issues in this chapter. As before, if it doesn't feel the right time for you to engage with these reflective questions and activities, leave them for when it does feel right. Make a note in your Reflective Journal about what didn't feel right and do something resourcing for yourself.

As you read through this chapter and the descriptions of some of the patterns that occur, did any of them resonate with you? If so, which ones? Did you identify with more than one of these relationships? What responses were stimulated in you, as you read?

Your pattern might be different to any of these, and if so, how would you describe the pattern you are caught in? What might be going on within it − do you recognise that you carry hope that it will one day be different or guilt that you want to be free from it?

Create your own 'case study' − take some time to ponder your own relationship with your mother and write about it in your journal, under your own title or one of those detailed in this chapter. Write it in the third person, as if you are describing someone else's experience, and let your imagination suggest what might be going on. In doing that, you can always come back and see what you want to take from it that is helpful and leave what isn't.

If you find it hard to write about this, you could always try to fictionalise the story, calling mother and daughter by different names, set in a different part of the country and having different family ties. Sometimes by taking this step away from the situation, it is possible to see it more clearly.

CHAPTER 8
The Continuing Cycle of Suffering;
Why it happens and How to Stop It

Between all the difficult relationship patterns I have outlined so far, you will notice similarities. For example, the rescuing daughter may act out of a sense of duty, and so too will the self-sacrificing daughter – these are different responses to the same root cause; similarly, becoming the parent as a way to manage a chaotic mother relationship could easily result in becoming a hurt daughter or an angry daughter. No wonder the web feels so constricting, as these threads bind us.

It may be hard for those who haven't experienced some of these more entangled relationships to understand why the daughters perpetuate these dynamics with their mothers. Many of the mothers in the scenarios I have outlined are experienced as being negative, demanding, narcissistic (that is, very self-absorbed), critical or envious of their daughters. Common themes for daughters are not being seen, not feeling wanted, loved or encouraged; not feeling good enough; feeling guilt and shame and feeling a burden. Why do daughters continue this cycle of suffering? It is a complex answer, if it were simple we would have all stopped doing it years ago, and the rest of the book seeks to add to the answer and offer some solutions.

Many of us might never have realised that a different way of relating was even possible, that it needn't be inevitable that we will be locked into this for life. We haven't even thought that we have choices. Caught up in that is the hope that I mentioned, that *'one day we will get the love and attention we have craved since childhood'*. Having hope is not always problematic but in these relationships it can be if it becomes magical thinking. These are thoughts that are wishes that can never come true as the solution is given to someone else, our mother. Other such thoughts are *'one day it will be my turn; if I work hard enough/do enough for her/others'*. If we hang onto these without question no change is possible.

We all carry this evolutionary fear of abandonment and may have experienced emotional or physical abandonment ourselves. Maybe we fear that to break free will lead us into exile, never having a relationship at all. This is the threat we might have felt keenly as a young child; that if we don't fit in with the unwritten rules in the family system or find a way to be the daughter our mothers can accept, we will be abandoned. We do whatever we can to avoid that possibility. If we have never experienced an emotional connection with our mother, or the person who is closest to us in early life, we do what we can to try to bridge the void and to connect in any way that is possible.

You may wonder why daughters don't get their needs for love met elsewhere. Well, some do, through creating loving partnerships and friendships or having loving relationships with their father or another close relative. However, these rarely replace or fill the emptiness of the loving bond we all long to have with our mother-figure. All human babies are born needing to love and to be loved. It is a fundamental primary need as an infant, along with nutrition, warmth, touch and safety. The focus for that love is the mother-figure and many of us grow up longing for it, if it has been denied us. We can spend our lives searching for it like a baby searching for a nipple or teat, because we have an inner space for an internalised loving mother which is empty or diminished.

If we have never experienced an emotional connection with our mother, or the person who is closest to us in early life, we continue to long for it

As we explored in Part 1, the web of entanglement is spun from the very beginning of our conception, meaning that through no fault of our own, we can be bound tightly to a mother who cannot, due to her own history, enable us to step fully into protecting ourselves. We have become stuck as victims within the dynamic. We might even feel that we don't deserve any better than this, having been programmed to believe this as a truth or having had our self-esteem diminished by our mother. Those who witness such entanglements in friends or relatives may find themselves thinking that change is easy, but it is not – otherwise daughters would surely make their lives easier. No, the nature of the tangled web means it is emotionally challenging and often distressing even to simply think of creating change, because this brings with it intense feelings of fear, guilt and shame.

We may have taken up a role in the family which we are

continuing in this relationship and maybe with others. If there was a risk of the family collapsing a young daughter might have taken on 'the organiser' role, she may continue this well into adulthood continuing to organise everything for her family, whether asked to or not. She may have become a successful organiser in her professional life but the entanglement with her family results in resentment and an ongoing demand on her time, and possibly, finances.

Another of the roles we might have been given or assumed is that of 'the rebel', we may have developed it as a way to annoy or manage a critical parent as a child. It could have become an identity we hold on to. We may have been called rebellious when we were younger, the term being a pejorative, and we may even continue to take delight in our rebelliousness as we get older. It could be that we weren't that rebellious as children at all, but simply wanted to be recognised for who we really were. We may have enjoyed being argumentative or delighted in developing a dress style that we knew would irk our mother, but this is all part of natural self-expression; how we develop our sense of self, and if it is belittled, then we feel belittled.

As we experimented with our style and values, our mother might have said, over and over, *"You are only doing this to be different, you look ridiculous."* Or *"You are only saying that to be different."* I bought an outfit last year that I knew my mother would have hated but I now know that it IS my taste and not simply a rejection of hers. If we rebelled or are still rebelling, it can be useful to explore whether we are rebelling against her control or are we on our own path to self-discovery? Do we feel a cruel delight to have annoyed her, and does doing that defend us from a fear that we might be like her after all? Have we given ourselves enough space and time to discover who we are and what we believe for ourselves, and ultimately what being ourselves really means? If not, this can be another part of the web we are caught up in.

Our responses to our relationship with our mother and the family context can become a way of life with other relationships and we may never question it. I took a sense of responsibility into the rest of my life, assuming responsibility for things I wasn't responsible for. I had a strong 'helper' motivation too, which is rescuing under a different name. This meant I was often overly helpful when it wasn't needed, and by so doing, I gave away time and energy that I could have used to improve my own life. And yet, as can be the case, these motivations – duty, responsibility, and helpfulness – led me towards a career in nursing, then teaching, and then psychotherapy, until with the help of my own therapist, I was eventually able to make sense of it for the first time.

The idea of the wounded healer is that those of us with wounds are attracted to trying to heal or save others, instead of focusing on our own wounds and saving ourselves. Rescuing, helping, feeling responsible and using work to prove our value (to whom, I now ask?) are part of the mix that can lead people into burnout, unless and until we stop and reflect about how this is working for us now we are adults, and whether the behaviour is giving us the outcomes we want for a healthy life.

The idea of the wounded healer is that those of us with wounds are attracted to trying to heal or save others, instead of focusing on our own wounds and saving ourselves

We have also taken in messages from the family and created our own thoughts about ourselves that hold us in these patterns of relationship. We have our own self-talk; those things we have been told about ourselves that we come to repeat. For example, I was talking with a friend recently who described herself as lazy. She is one of the least lazy people I know, so I suggested to her that this wasn't true and asked who had told her that. No surprises for guessing who – it was her mother, who had wanted her to stop reading or playing as a child, so she would do more around the house and take on the childcare of her younger siblings. We are easily programmable as young children as we are very open to sug-gestion and to what we are told about ourselves. If we track back some of our self-beliefs, as my friend did, we are likely to find they come from childhood. They are not 'givens' and we can change them. To do that we have first to become fully aware of them, bringing them out of the shadows of our unconscious habits.

Other thoughts many of us may carry deep within ourselves include:

- I am not good enough/I am not enough
- I must please people (or I won't be loved)
- I am responsible (for the feelings and behaviour of others)
- I must work hard and prove myself so I will be wanted
- I mustn't get things wrong, so I aim for perfection
- I don't deserve good things or happiness
- I need to be critical of myself or I will get complacent or above myself
- I am not lovable
- I must be independent, as no one will help me
- I can't trust people/everyone lets me down

- I must be strong/I mustn't show weakness
- I can't have what I want/I am not allowed to have what I want
- I must be a good daughter
- I mustn't betray my mother
- I must cling on as I can't cope on my own
- I should _____ I must _____ (fill in the gaps)

These all serve to hold our patterns in place; we have become locked into the story we have told ourselves. We need to identify them and challenge them, reframe them and replace them with healthier beliefs. I give some examples of this at the end of this chapter.

Perhaps we haven't developed the skills to stand up for ourselves in an authentic and assertive way, or we have but only use those skills outside the family. As children we might have been punished for speaking up, called cheeky or selfish or ignored. The punishment might have been more physical as well. We could have learnt to keep our heads down, suffer in silence and swallow our emotional needs. As an adult I often sensed my mother's vulnerability, and suspect I did as a child. I once tried to connect emotionally with what I saw as her vulnerability and was roundly rebuffed. Looking back, I can see I was very clumsy in how I handled it; I had suggested something to her about what she might be feeling. I think she felt, rightly, that I had no idea what she was feeling and the complexity of it all. At the time, my wounded child was activated and I was hurt. Developing our skills in this area can help us in all kinds of ways. Instead of jumping in rescuing we can ask, something like, *'what would you like to happen?'* or *'what would you like from me?'* The first time you do this you may not get the response you hope for but that doesn't mean that your approach is faulty, it means that you are changing the interaction. Alternatively, we can catch ourselves wanting to step closer to her and notice that without acting on it or being caught up in the hope that we can fill the gap.

Some daughters may decide to stop the game, put down the hope and any attempt at having a relationship with their mother. We may decide to exile ourselves for our own wellbeing and stop all contact with our mother. Whether we stay in contact or not, becoming disentangled requires us to face our fears of abandonment and of being in the world without our mother. We also need to attend, therapeutically, to whatever hurt or anger we may continue to carry. If we can face that, we have real choices. If we can't, then we remain caught in the 'there and then'. No change means more of the same.

For some daughters, where the relationship is destructive, it can be the best thing to step away from contact with our mother and to use that separation to focus on connecting with ourselves. This could bring a sense of healing, after which we may or may not wish to reconnect with our mother. I hear people say, *"But it's her mother..."* and this is true, but in some cases the mother may also be our persecutor and putting boundaries in place is an emotional lifesaver.

In some cases, the mother is also the persecutor and putting boundaries in place is an emotional lifesaver

It is up to us when it comes to making changes. We don't need anyone's permission and we don't need to justify it. For as long as we keep false hope alive and continue to think our mother should or shouldn't do something, we continue to be caught in the web. We can free ourselves through engaging with deep self-reflection and being helped by a good therapist or therapeutic coach or a self-development programme. Sometimes, we are blind to what is playing out within us, as we can't see it in ourselves until we look carefully and adjust our lens. That is why working with another is valuable, as they can act as a mirror, reflecting back our emotions to us and then we can notice what comes up in our relationship with them.

I had this experience recently in a reflective group. The question we were asked to consider was, 'What is absent within you?' My first response was, *"Well, if I knew that it wouldn't be absent,'* but by sitting with the question, I realised that what was absent was a sense of joy at having my deeper experiences heard and received by others without judgement. Instead, I felt a sort of dread. Many years ago, when I was training as a psychotherapist, we were taught that how we experience being in a group reflects something back to us about our childhood and how safe and loving it was. We were told that we all project our experience of our mother onto the group. This has always had a resonance with me. Certainly, our experience of being in a group in regard to how seen or liked or included or anxious we feel has some link to our early experiences and is a useful point of entry for enhancing our self-awareness. The question we may be asking ourselves is, *'How safe is it here to be authentically myself?'* Or *'Do I have to adapt here to be safe and not exiled?'* Groups like family systems have their own unconscious rules. If we can develop our self-belief and let go of our self-doubt, the fear of being exiled arising from the 'there and then' is not so active.

Spiral of Learning

Make a list of what comes to mind as being 3 or 5 things that keep you in the cycle of suffering. Choose one and imagine yourself letting that go. What happens when you do that?

Look back at the list of beliefs in this chapter, which of them, if any do you hold? Pick the 3 you recognise are most prevalent in your thinking.

What beliefs might you put in their place? For example:
- *'I am not good enough' can be replaced by 'I am good enough as I am'.*
- *'I must be strong' replaced by 'I can be strong at times, and it is okay for me to feel vulnerable and ask for help at other times'*
- *'I must be a good daughter' replaced by 'I can be the daughter I choose to be to my mother'*

List out any 'must, 'should', 'have to' thoughts you carry about your relationship with your mother. How might you turn that around? For example, 'I have to phone her weekly' to 'I will phone her weekly if I want to'.

CHAPTER 9
Supporting Learning and Change

The key hooks in our adult relationship with our mother are that we keep hoping next time things will be different or that if we are 'better daughters' this will make her respond to us differently. Or that if we keep punishing her, there will come a time when we feel free and good. These are false hopes.

Other false thinking is that we tell ourselves, *"She shouldn't do X or Y"* and complain about it repeatedly to ourselves and those around us. Thinking that people 'should be different' keeps us entangled with them. If our mother could be different, she would be – and what is more, we can't make her act in the ways we think she should. How she is, is how she is. That doesn't mean we have to like it or go back for more of it. If we can accept this, it is a step in the right direction and together with acceptance, we can find other techniques to help us move away from the tangled web. We probably have enough proof by now to know that things will just continue as they are unless we choose to make changes, and the first thing we need to do is explore the idea that we 'have to' continue in our relationship with our mother.

Thinking that people 'should be different' keeps us entangled with them

Mapping the interaction(s)

To raise our awareness of what is going on, we can map out the process of our interactions. I have imagined what might happen during a phone call where a daughter, lets call her Kitty, is entangled with her mother:

Action	Response
I think about phoning her	I feel I ought to I don't want to
I phone	I feel very reluctant I am on edge I am not relaxed
She tells me off for not phoning her sooner, the moment she answers	I feel she is berating me, and implying I am a bad daughter I just want her to say, "Hello Kitty, how lovely to hear from you", but she doesn't I hope she will
The game is now on... the habitual responses follow	
She tells me I obviously care more about my work than her	I had tried to use work as a reason for not phoning before That backfired on me

She tells me how lonely she is	It sounds accusatory to me I hear that as a dig, like a dagger going in It is my fault that she is lonely – my responsibility My heart sinks and I know 'the game' is well underway
I say I am sorry she is lonely	I actually feel exasperated with her I am not really sorry she is lonely I feel defeated I also want some real connection
She says no one cares about her	I am now emotionally pushed against the wall It is untrue, as I know my sister has phoned and her son I decide to change the subject
I tell her some of the highlights from my week	I hope this might spark a bit of interest I get nothing back
I ask her what she has been doing and she says a bit about her conversations and bridge	I hope this will work This feels safer territory I respond in a way I hope comes over as warm, but actually I am not really interested at all, just relieved we are on safer ground
She tells me she hasn't heard from my sons for a while	I feel this is my fault, Exasperation returns
We end the call	I feel like tearing my hair out
NEXT WEEK	We do it all again

Setting out the conversation like this shows 'the game' in action; that is, our mother's behaviour and how we interpret and respond to it. Before we know it maybe we feel accused, guilty and exasperated. The game that has started only has one ending. Setting it out this way might give you some insight into how you may be playing similar games. You can look back and see where the trip wires were and think about what you might do differently another time.

If you look through Kitty's example, and imagine it is yours, where might you start to make changes?

These are some of my first thoughts:
- The hope of *'this time it will be different and I will get the loving response I crave'* is present together with the anxiety that it will be as always. Perhaps Kitty would try to let go of that hope, knowing that her mother is likely to be the same as always. It may also help if Kitty phones at a time she feels calm and resourceful, so she is less vulnerable to the old triggers.
- Kitty could ignore the comment about loving work more than her mother. She doesn't have to justify herself
- Kitty could also have written out a card for herself with something like *'it is not my fault if she is lonely or feels uncared for, these are Mum's issues'*. She can then have it to hand to remind herself. She doesn't have to hear it as accusatory or take responsibility for it.
- *What would you add?*

We can see and probably recognise within ourselves, how quickly Kitty's feelings are stirred up and how she takes responsibility for her mother's situation.

Try mapping out the 'game' you are involved in with your mother. What do you notice? What thoughts about change come to mind?

Change won't just happen, we have to take responsibility for bringing it about. We might not get it right the first time or even the second, but each time we try gives us more feedback information to work with; it is all part of the learning.

Anger

It is understandable that some will feel angry at the mother's behaviour. Anger as an emotion can be a good thing, as it helps protect our boundaries and it rises when our boundaries are challenged or when we are disregarded. However, acting from a place of anger can be harmful. It may be something we choose to do to protect ourselves from attack, but it rarely creates the outcome we want in our relationship with our mother. Our anger can come out as cruelty, we may intentionally set out to hurt her. Acting to hurt or punish our mother is not stepping out of the tangled web, it is keeping it firmly in place. Many are afraid of anger and many daughters say, "*I hate the fact I am angry.*" They want to deny it or push it away, unless it is processed it will stay like a knot within us. We need to get to know our anger, not run away from it or let it consume us.

We need to use our anger with wisdom; that is, using it to raise our awareness of whether the anger is truly in the 'here and now' or whether it is 'there and then' anger from when our boundaries were disregarded as children? If it is the latter, acting from that place means we are still stuck in the web. We can also become more aware of what we do with our anger. Like many, I mostly re-press and swallow mine down and as a result, it often comes out as tears and sadness. When I look deeper, I find a lingering sense of rage that I have not dealt with.

Acting to hurt or punish our mother is not stepping out of the tangled web, it is keeping it firmly in place

Take responsibility
Our first step is to take responsibility for our part of the suffering we experience and for changing our patterns of relating. This includes recognising any magical thinking or false hope that operates within us and becoming aware of what triggers us and how we respond.

Making space for reflection and connection with yourself
We need to make space to reflect and digest what comes up within us in relation to our mother and to reading this book. By connecting with our body, emotions and thoughts, and being with what emerges, we can bring this more into our awareness where we can reflect on and explore them. Reflection enables us to observe ourselves and digest our experience. This process leads to learning and wisdom, which in turn enables us to change.

We can't change the past but we can change the present and therefore the future

Compassion and Letting Go of Blame

It is important for us to remember that our mothers were not born this way and it isn't our fault they have made the life choices they have or behave towards us as they do. They have their own relationship history from childhood and their own sense of not being seen, loved, wanted and protected as a child. They have developed these defensive ways of relating to survive being in relationships. They are relating in the only way they can. We can be compassionate towards them whilst also not taking responsibility for them, instead focusing on our part in the web and what we can do to change that. If we can allow compassion to arise, we can let go of blame. This isn't the same as pretending that we haven't been hurt by our mother's behaviour. Becoming stuck in blaming her doesn't help free ourselves from the tangled web. We can hold her to account for her behaviour while also not having a blaming narrative constantly running.

Becoming aware of how we tell our stories can offer some insights, do we focus them on our mother: *"She is this, she does that"*? Or do we focus on ourselves and how we feel and think? The former keeps us stuck. The latter helps us grow wisdom. Reflecting on our part of the web will not always be comfortable, that is alright, it is part of the process. What is important is that we draw on compassionate enquiry, that is without judgement, self-blame or guilt.

Take out your Reflective Journal and write for 30 minutes or so about what has come up for you in reading these chapters. Or use the tool of 'image creating' to do that with coloured pens and paper.

Part 4 tells you how to shift from an unhealthy, entangled relationship to a healthy one. The next Part takes you further into understanding what lies behind the emotional needs that lead to entanglement.

PART 3

GETTING TO THE HEART OF IT: EMOTIONAL TRAUMA

Personal Reflection (3)

I remember being in a therapy group quite some time ago now, when I had the deep realisation that much of my childhood experience had been unhappy, it was like running full pelt into a wall. I saw the truth for the first time. I had known it all my life of course but hadn't seen it or acknowledged it.

The few photographs that exist from my childhood show smiling people, a garden, the beach. In one I am sitting next to my father with a huge smile on my face. Were these a lie or was the therapy wrong? I know there are some who believe that you should leave the past alone and that no good will come from revisiting it. That puts most of psychotherapy out of business and leaves us with an undigested past, like a weight in our gut.

I chose to revisit my past and I found this split in myself between the unhappy aspects of my childhood and the moments where there was connection, like sitting next to my father on a visit to Dartmoor. Both feelings are true. I know I can't change my past but unless I recognise its truth, I can't change how it continues to reverberate in my life now: the fights I am still carrying on, the illusions or escape hatches I keep going through which take me into behaviour which doesn't do me any good, like over-working or berating myself or doubting myself. My parents were good people who were caught in the web of history and circumstance having come through a world war. They did what they could to give me a childhood that would enable me to become an independent adult.

I can't change my past but unless I recognise its truth, I can't change how it continues to reverberate in my life now

CHAPTER 10
What is Emotional Trauma?

At the heart of any entangled or difficult relationship with our mother is emotional trauma.

The term trauma can cause alarm, but it is part of the human condition. Understanding it is a way of growing through it. Avoiding exploring it however, is to stay locked within the negative consequences it has for us and our lives. I use the term emotional trauma here, but you may have seen it characterised elsewhere as attachment and developmental trauma. These are just different terms for describing how our early experience affects us.

Few children grow up without any trauma, as parenting is difficult and life can be challenging. Babies and children are vulnerable and being alive involves constantly responding to our changing environment. For some children, the effect on them is more intense as the situation they were born into makes huge emotional demands on them. Due to our dependency on our main care giver, how they related to, and cared for us has a lasting impact. We are also affected by the behaviour of family members, those in our close community and by any distressing life experiences we suffer.

Many adults are additionally traumatised by what is sometimes referred to as 'shock trauma', this includes domestic and sexual abuse, serving in the armed forces, being caught up in a terrifying event, being a refugee or suffering conflict. Racial abuse, being demonised for being part of a particular social group, and the stress of poverty are also traumatising. We live in a traumatising society.

Emotional trauma is so widespread and is my focus in discussing our relationships with our mothers. The rapid development of neuroscience over the last twenty years has changed our understanding about how we respond to our childhood experience. We are the first group of daughters who can make use of this knowledge to bring about changes in our lives. In our mother's childhood it was widely assumed by professionals and society that children were resilient and there was no impact on them from the myriad scenarios I have referred to in previous chapters. Childhood sexual abuse wasn't really recognised, nor its consequences, until the 1970s; even then the scale of it wasn't appreciated. Domestic abuse was of course known about by those affected but it was largely seen as a 'family or domestic matter' and the impact remained unrecognised.

Trauma is the lasting impact of our experiences on our nervous system, our brain, the cells in our body and our emotions. It occurs when our nervous system, that senses danger, has been overwhelmed by the effect on us of the behaviour of others or the circumstance we are in. It is held within us. The greater our exposure to traumatising experience, the greater the impact as it is cumulative. If we are not helped to process and digest this experience the responses stay within us, largely in our unconscious, influencing and providing our reactions to situations in the present. This is the 'there and then' operating in the 'here and now'.

Trauma is the lasting impact of our experiences on our nervous system, our brain, the cells in our body and our emotions

It is this internal state that is active in difficult relationships with our mother, and when we are unloving of ourselves. In such contact with our mother there are two internal trauma states entangled with each other that I call the tangled knotted web: hers and ours. Together they create the chasm that separates us and the dynamics that bind us and are full of unacknowledged and undigested history. By undigested, or unprocessed, I refer to the emotions which have stayed locked away, maybe frozen and numb, whilst continuing to influence our conscious awareness. Defrosting them or bringing them back into life and caring lovingly for them, means that they can become fully part of us, adding to our capacity for living in the present, rather than repeating the past. It is like when we defrost food which then nourishes us. It takes a lot of energy to keep things frozen, whether that be food or emotions.

Unknotting and unravelling the web involves understanding the possible causes of our pain, developing our self-awareness of the signs and symptoms of the web in action in the present, and working with them to achieve resolution within us. This includes changing patterns in how we relate to our mother and to ourselves.

It takes a lot of energy to keep things frozen, whether that be food or emotions

Understanding how trauma operates within us needs curiosity and self-reflection. Keeping a reflective journal can stimulate our awareness of our own habitual patterns of relating to others and ourselves and to explore what lies beneath them. We may start with considering a recent exchange with our mother, or another which felt entangled or difficult. This will help us to become aware of any behaviour or thought patterns that were operating within us (such as rescuing or feeling responsible). If we go deeper in our inner enquiry we may find feelings of anxiety, agitation, vulnerability, rage, shame, terror, fear of abandonment or of being hurt.

The main causes of emotional trauma are:

- Being unable to process emotional responses to distressing and overwhelming life events or circumstances, either because we were too immature to be able to, or because those around us weren't able to help us to do that, or because it was so overwhelming. These responses are likely to emerge in unpredictable ways. Such experiences include caesarean and difficult births, illness, loss and separation and the many factors raised in Part 1.
- Feeling unloved by those closest to us. This is a body-based sensation, not a thinking one and can result in us not loving ourselves or feeling emotionally abandoned
- Feeling unwanted from the beginning and/or not feeling wanted for ourselves later in life. This can lead us to not wanting or honouring ourselves
- Being unprotected and exposed to abuse. We may not have learnt how to protect ourselves or our capacity to trust others is diminished

Psychologist Professor Franz Ruppert ('*Trauma, Fear and Love*' *2014*) identifies our fundamental human needs as being to be wanted, to be loved and protected. If these go unmet, he says, the trauma response is activated within us. Thomas Hübl, who also teaches about trauma, talks of our fundamental needs as being 'to be allowed to be, to belong and to become (fully ourselves)'. If we did not feel loved, wanted or protected, our ability to be, belong and become is also violated.

I explore these more deeply in the next chapters, linking the causes with the possible lasting effects. The messages we pick up from our care-givers are carried in their voice tone, what they say, what emotions they express towards us, how they hold or touch us, and in their facial expressions and their eyes. They may say '*of course I wanted or loved you*' but we may not have always felt that or experienced it from their behaviour and how they cared for us.

Maybe you feel you are not affected by any emotional trauma, and you regularly experience excitement, creative energy, compassion and vitality. If so, I hope that this part of the book will be valuable in helping you understand the behaviour of others and to support them as a friend. It might be that you have a good enough relationship with your mother but become aware that you carry emotional trauma which affects you in other ways.

They may say 'of course I wanted or loved you' but we may not have always felt that or experienced it from their behaviour and how they cared for us.

There are four elements of the theoretical understanding that can help us make more sense of emotional trauma:

- Our nervous system, cells and memory banks store everything from conception onwards, including experiences that we can't recall in visual or auditory memory. Our birth is an example of this.
- The impact of experience is so significant in infants and children because our brains are immature and as a result respond instantly to threats to survival; for example, to the absence of the mother.
- Our brains develop, together with the response pathways we lay down, through our relationships with those close to us.
- As children we can't defend ourselves, psychologically or physically, and we have nowhere to go. We are powerless and totally dependent on those around us for food, shelter, safety and our physical and emotional wellbeing.

The interplay between these is why we are so vulnerable as children; emotional trauma is so widespread. As you will know, how brain development and memory works is the subject of many books. For our purposes, I have highlighted factors that I hope help us understand our own experiences, in particular in relation to our mother and ourselves. The bibliography lists further reading on this subject.

We are all familiar with recall memory: *"I remember when..."* type of narrative that we create from the sensory responses at the time of the experience. This can be distorted by perception and the meaning we give it at the time and afterwards, so is never a 'true' record. However, it is our memory of *our* experience. Daughters may have been told they made things up and had their experience disregarded or disbelieved. We may have had an active imagination, but we know in our bodies what our experience was.

Some mothers are characterised as 'reinventing history' – trying to put in place a version of what happened to meet their own needs for denial or forgiveness or to create an idealised version of the past. Although we may need to be open to reviewing our memory as it isn't always an accurate or complete version of what happened, and it can become distorted, most daughters know if what is presented by their mother is at odds with their own recall and felt experience, that is what they feel in their body. If we have been told as children that a memory is wrong, or if we are vulnerable to the judgement of others, things can get confusing, as our inner experience differs from what we are being told by another.

How much we can recall varies widely. For example, I have huge gaps in my memory whereas my brother seems to have an elephant's memory of our past. The more intense or different the experience the deeper the memory tends to be; at the same time, intense experience can lead to a 'blanking out' of recall memory. Some of us may recall things very clearly, both good and bad experiences.

Recall memory doesn't start until we have language, around the age of two years old and may not do so in some circumstances after that, another type of memory will have been and remains potentially active in our lives all the time. It is this other form of memory, called implicit memory which, when activated in the present brings the 'there and then' responses into the 'here and now'. It responds immediately to triggers; talking with our mother can be an example of when this happens. These emotional memory pathways are felt in our bodies and therefore, part of our self-reflection on an interaction with our mother, or another, can helpfully include asking ourselves, *"What do I feel in my body?"*. Sometimes, connecting with our body in this way also brings an association or a memory or an image. We can explore all these responses and note them in our journal.

The bulk of our memory storage is this implicit memory. It is vast, like a huge internet server, with innumerable networked pathways. This is why our earliest experience of being in our mother's womb, of birth and our early years, and many other experiences continue to resonate within us even though we have no recall memory. This memory bank also carries experiences of feeling safe, loved and happy where they were present in our lives. These can also be triggered by experiences in the 'here and now'.

If we link this type of memory with how our immature brain responds to external signs of danger, we can see how it holds information regarding our feelings of lack of safety, danger and fear of abandonment. Using separation from the mother as an example, to the infant's brain this feels as dangerous as if the mother has died. Watch any young animal and you will see the anxiety they feel when the mother is out of sight. Such early separations or break in loving contact are not held in the recall memory. As older children we may remember separations and our emotional responses, for example, if we were in hospital.

It is not unusual for babies to have to be cared for in an incubator for a few days, weeks, or months after birth. This usually follows a difficult or premature birth or if the baby needs specialised treatment. This separation is highly stressful and traumatising for the baby. The impact may stay within the daughter as she grows up, she may be clingy with some partners and scared of being left, she may recognise she fears abandonment. The separation from the mother may also affect the developing relationship between the two. Many may not realise that this has left a legacy and it can be helpful to consider it as part of understanding of ourselves.

Whilst this is not a pure science, we can sometimes match possible inputs to the outputs of our emotional trauma. We don't need to be able to make clear connections to digest our experience. We know we have the trauma within us from the signs and symptoms that we experience in the present and we can work with those to process what is stuck within us.

In early trauma or where the emotional or physical pain is so intense, the recall memory of images and sounds are not laid down. Some women who were sexually abused as children may have no recall memories and can be confused by their responses in the present which appear to have no cause. This can be the case for all other experiences of emotional trauma. The intrinsic memory can be highly activated in the present by situations that mirror the past. Some women's unconscious memories of sexual abuse can be activated if they have a vaginal examination or go to the dentist or when giving birth.

Another protective process is that the nervous system shuts down the feedback from the body to the brain, thus blocking out the sensations of pain from the body. This helps us survive at the time. Unfortunately, this separation deepens and as adults we may find it hard to have an internal sense of what we are experiencing. We can develop ways of overcoming this and building up our connection with our inner felt experience. We can build up new pathways that allow this to happen.

We may use recall memory to drive change, for example, by thinking, *"I am never going to let that happen to my children"*, or *"I am always going to do that for my children."* Memories help us learn from experience if we reflect on them and decide what action we want to take. If we did have mothering that hurt us, we may take steps not to mother our children in the same way. Nevertheless, we still have our own emotional processing work to do and until then, our unconscious emotional memories may affect our relationships.

Memories we keep secret rather than share usually carry a high emotional charge, including shame. The secret-holder might be afraid that if the experience were to be spoken of, the emotion would overwhelm her. This can be the case for memories of physical and sexual abuse. Secrets can have a toxic effect on us as they are active within us – both the experience and the need to keep it hidden. Many women are ashamed to talk of having been abused and try to push any memories right out of their awareness, hoping that it won't affect them in the present. Unfortunately, that is not what happens. It is healthier for us if we can find a trustworthy person to tell our secret to when we feel able. It means we can begin to deal with whatever emotions are locked up with it and find some release from the past's hold over us.

Memories we keep secret rather than share usually carry a high emotional charge, including shame

Stories rather than memories

Sometimes we are told stories by our mother or other family members about us as babies and children, along with the underlying or overt message that goes with them. These can be loving stories that reinforce how loved and wanted we feel, or ones that serve to tell us how difficult we were found to be. With the latter, the focus of the story is often about the impact of our behaviour as an infant or child on someone else. Any compassion for us tends to be absent. When told these stories as children, we absorb the message and then often do what we can to 'make up' for the apparent effects of our behaviour.

Having a baby who cries a lot can be very disturbing for a mother who may resort, out of desperation, to putting the baby down the bottom of the garden or in a room with the door closed and leaving her there for some time. Some mothers choose to tell their daughters all this and say something like *"You cried for six months when you were born, and it was very difficult time for me"*. The message is very clear: that you, the baby, were at fault and difficult, and the story has become part of the family system of myths and legends. What is the daughter to make of it, though? As a child hearing the story, she may internalise that she ruined her mother's life and wasn't a lovable baby. As a result, she might have spent her whole life trying to make up to her mother for it.

At the level of her own implicit memory, though, what of the infant's experience of being put in a dark room as a distressed baby of a few days old? It will have been stressful being separated from her mother and getting no comfort or loving touch. The markers for that are in her nervous system and implicit memory. Anyone who has been a mother knows how difficult it is to have a baby who can't be soothed. However, it is not the baby's fault that she cries a lot, nor in most cases is it the mother's. Maybe the mother feels some guilt and tells the story to relieve that, shifting the blame from her to her daughter who may pick it up. Now she is an adult, the daughter can consider the story differently and see that she was a helpless, distressed baby that no one comforted at the time. She didn't ruin her mother's life and she can let go of that story. She can learn how to be a loving comforting mother to herself now she is an adult.

Narrating our Life

Most of us develop well-told stories about our life, based on recall memory. Such stories can be positively or negatively reinforcing, often they may be self-deprecating. These stories may not include the associated emotional content, or when we tell them we may become overtaken, again, by feelings of helplessness or sorrow. We can all become aware of how we narrate our life, including the stories we tell about ourselves and our mother or us as children.

I came to realise that I told stories about my mother, often about adult interactions, which put me in the 'poor me' role and I decided to stop doing this as they kept me locked into the narrative. The more I stopped using these, the more I noticed good memories emerging. My storytelling had stopped these good memories from being present, as in some ways they conflicted with the story I was hanging on to. I needed to do the self-reflective work that would free me from them. For some, I realise, there may not be any or many good memories in the first place, but it is healing to recognise those there are, however few.

The more I stopped using these narratives and took responsibility for myself as an adult, the more I noticed good memories emerging

With emotional trauma, we can carry anxiety, fear, terror, shame, rage, a sense of vulnerability, and/or a fear of abandonment in our implicit memory. These emerge, sometimes in confusing ways, when something in the present reminds our nervous system of traumatising experiences in the past – and we find we have just reacted without engaging our adult mind. We can practise allowing a space between the stimulus (perhaps something our mother says or does) and our response. We can take some deep breaths, breathing in and out slowly, taking an emotional 'step backwards' and considering how, as adults, we now want to respond. This helps us break free of patterns from childhood. Most of us start doing this reflection after the event, but as we practise, we get better at doing it in the moment.

Being able to regulate our emotional state is another helpful practice, limiting any tendency we have towards too few emotional filters and moderating our impulse to react. Many of us who carry emotional trauma are less able to regulate our breathing and stress levels as this wasn't modelled to us by our mothers because they, too, had limited capacity for that themselves. We can learn it now. The key to self-regulation is through deep breathing exercises and slowing a racing mind, which prevents us from becoming overwhelmed.

Spiral of Learning

If in reading this, you were affected emotionally, do go and do something resourcing for yourself, maybe talking to a friend or going for a walk or doing something practical.

Are there stories told about you as a baby that imply you had a negative impact on your mother or those around you? How might these affect you in the 'here and now'? How could you reframe them? For example, you might reframe the narrative of "I ruined my mother's life" to "I was a distressed baby". Sticking with a mother's narrative that "I ruined her life" may lead to behaviour designed to correct that or make up for it; such behaviour entangles a daughter with her mother.

Reflecting on experiences in the present and the impacts on us, takes us into stored experiences from the past. When writing in your Reflective Journal, ask yourself some questions:
- *What did I feel or notice in my body? Anything or nothing?*
- *What emotions arise as I sit with the experience? Do I feel numb?*
- *What about in my mind? What memories, stories or thoughts arise?*

If you have secrets or memories with intense emotions, I recommend that you seek help from someone who can hear your story and help you digest it.

CHAPTER 11
Why Being and Feeling Loved Matters

A mother's love matters for our emotional development and capacity to love ourselves. Loving ourselves means that we take care of ourselves, we pay attention to our needs and take healthy action to meet them; we rest when we need to and play when we can. While love from our father and others close to us is also important, it does seem to be the case that a primary need of a child is to feel wanted and loved by her mother. We are primed to love our mother unconditionally and long for that from her. This desire for a loving bond has an evolutionary survival basis as we need to have all our needs for food, warmth, safety, touch and play met by those closest to us.

Many new mothers report falling in love with their babies and this is aided by the production of the hormone oxytocin within the mother. This is sometimes called 'the love hormone', although it has many other valuable functions. A loving connection occurs when a mother is tuned into her daughter's emotional, physical, and relational needs. Remember Scenario 1 in Chapter 1: where the mother keeps constant eye contact with her baby, as well as gentle touch and soothing facial expressions and maybe baby-talk or toys to entertain or engage her daughter? The mother is calmly present, giving her daughter her full attention, both sensing and seeing her. She takes joy in her. Her daughter takes joy in her mother too and she develops her own memory sensations of being seen and loved. From this arises the feeling that we are lovable.

Many factors can interrupt, disrupt, or inhibit this loving attunement and connection from the mother: if our mother was stressed, agitated or distracted; perhaps she was overwhelmed by being a mother or by having another child; perhaps she suffered postnatal depression or was coping with difficult, challenging or even dangerous circumstances – as a result, her attention is elsewhere and not on us. She may carry shame or guilt which in turn will affect how she mothers us. Mothers may struggle to connect emotionally and to care physically for their babies. For some mothers, love of their daughter, or of others, is difficult because they have never, or only briefly, experienced it for themselves as children.

Infants focus on their mother's face, eyes and voice. We experience love by looking into our mother's eyes, seeing her love there and feeling it in our body in how she holds us. Our first mirror is our mother's eyes then additionally in the eyes and faces of those who care for us. We develop our sense of ourselves through these relationships. The nervous systems of the mother and daughter are in resonance with each other. If our mother was calm most of the time, that will transfer itself to us. If she looks at us lovingly we feel seen and wanted.

Our first mirror is our mother's eyes then additionally in the eyes and faces of those who care for us

If we don't see love or feel it in how we are held and handled, this is experienced as life threatening by our immature nervous system and is stored in our intrinsic memory as emotional trauma. This starts early in our life. It is likely that if our mother found it hard to connect lovingly with us enough of the time, that will continue throughout our relationship. It might be that the love is conditional in relation to how we behave as children and adults and therefore the love has become distorted. In response, we do what we can to make ourselves lovable by adapting. However, this doesn't change the conditionality of the love. When we acknowledge that it is impossible for mothers to be all loving all the time, it is easy to see how all babies can feel these shocks. We can also appreciate that for some children, their danger response can be more highly activated, more often.

Love also influences how our brains develop. We are social beings, shaped by our earliest relationships which in turn are affected by the context of our lives. Our brains and sense of ourselves develop through the quality of interaction with those closest to us. We also need play and stimulation. This doesn't require expensive toys but playful interaction with our mother or others, the use of colourful objects and encouragement to develop our hand and recognition skills. Some mothers are able to play with their daughters as they were played with as children or have developed that capacity in adulthood. Other mothers are less able or unable to be playful. They haven't had the opportunity to learn how to play, or their anxiety and stress levels, or demands on them are too great to relax into playfulness or perhaps, their neurodiversity prevents this being possible. Perhaps the rules of the family system see play as a waste of time or frivolous. This may leave a legacy of not being able easily to access playfulness in ourselves. We can learn how to be playful adults, once we move beyond the self-limiting thoughts or behaviour patterns that have prevented this from happening.

Through our relationships, play and stimulation, we develop our higher brain which can assess situations, make decisions, and gives us our sense of our own autonomy and agency; our capacity to lead our own life. Our higher brain also develops our capacity to be social animals, to cooperate and empathise with others. We use this part of our brain to manage our emotions and impulses, to reassure ourselves about how safe (or not) the present is, even if our old responses are behaving as if it is dangerous, and whether to act if we need to protect ourselves. It is also where our ability for self-awareness and reflection comes from. These functions can be poorly developed in children who had an impoverished childhood. We can enhance our capacity for self-reflection and for developing our agency, that is, our capacity for self-direction and guidance, over our lifetime; but first we need to recognise that we need and want to do this.

As children we can get loving connection from others, from fathers, grandparents, step- or adoptive mothers, who show us love and play with us and provide safe havens. From such experiences we take in the sensations of being loved and seen. They can all make us feel special. Grandmothers may offer a safe space and many daughters will remember cakes being baked and the loving attention they received. Likewise, fathers can be tender and reassuring, involving us in a wide range of activities which feeds our feeling of being loved and seen.

However healthy our other attachments may be, the one with

our mother usually remains deeply important. If a mother leaves the family and the daughter has a close bond with her father and step-mother, the daughter can still long for something from her mother even though that was never forthcoming. The daughter may experience her mother as never making space for her or attending to her lovingly, and yet, she continues to hope that one day it will be different. The child's need for love and recognition from her mother and not getting it can have a lasting impact into adult life.

The myth that all mothers instinctively love their children unconditionally, are always willing to meet their children's needs and are selfless in their devotion makes it near impossible for mothers to admit if this isn't their experience. Instead, they feel shame and possibly even more resentment. Many mothers experience hatred for their baby at some time. This might be a flash of hatred amongst lots of loving kindness. This maternal ambivalence, the swing between love and hatred is normal and to be expected, as babies are demanding and life changing, and mothers aren't saints. However, women know how society treats those who don't live up to the idealised myths of motherhood. They can experience disdain and horror from others or be treated as if mentally unbalanced. If part of them has wished at times for the child to die or has wanted to hurt the child, they carry the shame evoked and imagine it makes them a bad mother. It silences them and so they struggle alone. Many mothers can't bear the shame, so they push it out of their conscious awareness while blaming the baby for not being lovable, thus increasing the hatred and resentment. This produces a vicious cycle which ensnares the daughter who senses and sees the hatred in the mother's eyes and this produces the danger response and emotional trauma. Post-natal depression is a more severe form of this ambivalence, where the mother finds it hard to connect with her infant at all and is overwhelmed by the experience of being a mother.

We may never know the extent of our mother's ambivalence, if she experienced it, and how well able she was to handle it within herself. However, we may well have the symptoms of emotional trauma from our experience of it; perhaps we don't quite trust her, or don't feel safe with her. This may extend to other women we meet at work or in social contexts. Something about them reminds us of our 'there and then' experience of not feeling safe, and we may have become super-sensitive to any indicators of hate, dislike or rejection. These might not really be present, but just something about the woman's face, voice or demeanour triggers our early nervous system responses. We may find we respond negatively to such women, perhaps feeling anxious and agitated. We may also find it hard to be supported by other women at work or in our wider lives.

Many mothers are able to tolerate their ambivalence, with love being predominant. Their love is firm enough not to be challenged if their daughter pushes them away or won't be comforted. If, occasionally, her momentary hatred does stimulate distress, her love quickly switches back on, and she reassures her daughter. The moment passes and her daughter feels safe again. A loving family with a minimum of stress and anxiety and good supportive friends makes it more possible for such a mother to manage this well.

However, if a mother unconsciously carries her own inner conflicts, pain and fear from childhood or the present, she is one of those least able to tolerate her ambivalent feelings for her daughter. She is also likely to remain unaware of the nature of her conflicting feelings for the baby, thus blaming the daughter, in which case the balance of love and hate may tip towards hate, with consequent implications for the emotional trauma of the daughter.

Some daughters are, in effect, emotionally abandoned by their mothers who find expressing love difficult or who are ill or are overwhelmed by emotional demands. Our physical needs may continue to be met, and to many on the outside, all might look 'normal'. Maybe our experience was: *"Mum looked after us practically, but I can't honestly say she mothered us."*

If a mother unconsciously carries her own inner conflicts, pain and fear from childhood, she is one of those least able to tolerate her ambivalent feelings for her daughter

Some daughters may also be physically neglected, particularly if the mother is ill or has an addiction. They may have been scared as children and tried to protect and care for any younger siblings including finding food for them; they may have had no one to turn to.

While most of us remain dependent on a parent or parents until late adolescence, or even later, some daughters had to learn to be independent very early in life, particularly those who were emotionally and physically abandoned. Some daughters' childhoods end early through having to take on adult practical tasks. Rarely, children may be forced to steal food and move around for shelter. Where children are emotionally and physically abandoned by adults, they may find it harder to connect emotionally with their daughter as their own emotional development had been so under-resourced as a child. No one was there to protect her or care for her and she had to become frozen emotionally to survive. This emotional freezing can be felt by her daughter.

Children who don't experience a loving environment often talk about 'shutting down' their emotional needs and extent of their connection with others. This is a survival response to trauma; it helps them continue to live, despite the lack of loving connection, but at the same time, their creativity and capacity for play is also shut down. Emotional abandonment is deeply painful for a child. We can often see in some of our mothers' histories that they were emotionally abandoned by their parents. Such a child finds all kinds of ways of surviving, perhaps becoming very independent, unwilling to trust others, emotionally unavailable herself and carrying that unmet need into her adult life and relationships. She may also feel she *'isn't enough'*, as though if she had been, her mother would have loved her, or that *'there isn't enough love or space for her'* and this sense of scarcity can be taken into other spheres including her work life.

To survive, we needed to adapt to the care we are given. We choose adaptation attachment over authenticity, that is, becoming fully ourselves. This adaptation includes taking on roles, like 'mother's little helper' or 'the rescuer' or striving not to be any trouble in the hope of getting love. We continue such roles into adulthood, paticularly rescuing – being the heroic saviour, or the 'martyr' or 'the caretaker'. We can also take these roles and survival defences into our work life, perhaps through overworking (in the hope of getting love and recognition and to push away painful emotions), or becoming a wounded healer, draining ourselves of all energy in the process. If our needs for loving connection go unmet, we carry a longing for it until we recognise what we are doing and realise that looking for it in these ways doesn't work. We come to recognise that the emotional cost to us is too great. Resentment also builds up as we can think, *"Look at all I do for you, and you still won't love me."*

It can be challenging to realise deep down that we were emotionally abandoned, not because we were unlovable but because it was tough for our mother to love us in the way we needed as infants and children. However, if we resonate with this as having some truth for us, we can be open to how that plays out in our adult lives. We can also create space and capacity to love ourselves. We can stop trying to entangle others into loving us. This includes relinquishing this expectation from our mother who may not have the capacity to love us freely. We need to stop hoping that one day she will.

The way out is to love ourselves. This is tough for many of us, but unless we develop the capacity to do this – which takes practise and doesn't just happen overnight – we cannot free ourselves from our tangled web of emotional trauma that entangles us with our mother.

Spiral of Learning

If there is something in this chapter that has disturbed you, go and do something that is resourcing for you. Choose an activity that will help calm you and bring light into your life right now. This is an example of loving yourself.

Notice with whom, when and where you felt loved – in your bones, not in your head. Treasure it and allow that unconditional love into your inner self. Write out the story from that time, put in as many details as you remember, really feel the love and safety you experienced.

If it feels right for you, use your Reflective Journal to explore what has struck you or come up for you as you read this chapter. Has any new insight arisen? Or has it left you feeling numb or a bit agitated? Where do you feel that in your body? If the latter, what associations or images, come up and what characteristics are carried by them?

If you recognise you had a loving connection from early on with your mother, treasure it; be that loving presence in the lives of others.

If you recognise that you didn't have a loving connection with your mother, what deep self-beliefs are linked with that? For example, 'I don't feel lovable'. As before, how might you reframe those beliefs? For example: 'I don't feel lovable' to 'I didn't feel my mother's love but I know I am lovable as a person'.

CHAPTER 12
Being Wanted for Who You Are

From our mothers we take in our sense of being wanted from the moment we are conceived and then as a baby and later, for who we are. We can also take this in from our fathers. If we don't feel wanted, we sense a danger to our survival which results in emotional trauma. If we take in the sensations and voiced messages that we are not wanted, we can end up not wanting ourselves or prioritising our own lives. We can stop seeing who we are behind the adaptations we have put in place to survive. Our ability to 'be' and 'to become' are inhibited.

Many mothers want their daughters and relish the child's developing personality and talents. They encourage the expression of our uniqueness and take pleasure in our talents. They support their daughters when they experiment with how they want to express themselves in the world. At times they will find us challenging, but that is part of a loving relationship and we both learn through that. This chapter, however, explores what happens when we feel we are not wanted or recognised for who we are and what we have achieved. It provides another piece of the jigsaw of understanding emotional trauma cause and effect.

Contrary to popular mythology, many women actively choose not to conceive or give birth. Other women do not make an active choice about parenting, but it becomes part of their life journey nonetheless, though a proportion of them did not want to have children at that time, or ever. Such women do not provide welcoming homes in their womb for the growing infant. This is not to deny that there are many who are delighted to be pregnant, engage with the infant immediately and make room in their lives for the baby. But, for some mothers, the conditions of their lives are such that they are not able to respond to their pregnancy and new baby in the way they might wish if things were different externally, or in their psyche.

Several daughters didn't have children as they didn't want to repeat the mother/daughter dynamic they had experienced or didn't trust themselves as mothers. Some might have thought, "I want this to stop with me", a sort of heroic gesture, as if the daughter wasn't capable of being a good mother to her child. Some of them, like me, didn't have opportunities either, but neither did we create them. I hear some childless daughters say, "I'm not the maternal kind", which may be a healthy assessment of themselves, or a way of protecting themselves. Being clear about whether we want to be a mother or not is important. Many women are fulfilled in their lives without children. Others may carry regrets about not having had children, whilst some may get their mothering needs met through caring for the children of others.

Not all women want to have children and it is part of the myth of motherhood to pretend otherwise. If you google 'women who don't have children', much of what you find is about fertility. Of course, there are women whose ambitions to conceive and become pregnant were sadly not fulfilled, naturally or by other means, where the issue is fertility or life opportunity. However, the general impression about not having children centres on the factor of fertility rather than choice, which reinforces the illusion that all women want to have children. It also denies the reality that for some women, the conditions of their lives and the relationships they are in, are not appropriate for having a child.

The widely held expectation that all women want children leaves many in a very difficult position. Women who don't have children are subtly excluded from many arenas where mothers and their babies come together, either because they are working, or the understandable focus of mothers on their babies leaves little room in the conversation for other matters. Childless women can also be looked down upon and pitied for their choices. Being a mother brings with it social prestige. I am sure many of you who have given birth and been through the tough early months of mothering would tell me there is no social prestige. However, daughters who don't have children often feel fed up that being a mother always trumped not being a mother in their family, and wider society. They additionally may have experienced the expectation that they should be the one to do more for their parents than a sister who has children.

It is perfectly understandable that an unconscious or conscious motive for having a baby may be to belong to that club, thus proving your fertility and claim to the important role of motherhood in society. It is also understandable that some women may feel huge pressure to join in, when parts of them really don't want children at all, or at least, not now, or not so many. Some researchers estimate that one in four pregnancies are not wanted, with many ending in termination, where that option is available. In earlier generations and in some cultures where termination of a pregnancy was not available, unwanted pregnancies continued and infanticide – the killing of the infant or failure to keep it alive – may have occurred. Before abortion was legal, there were many failed attempts at termination, when women tried to end the pregnancy themselves and maybe didn't succeed. The infant carries the impact of that act in her body and how she relates to her daughter. Sometimes the mother might have told the daughter that a termination had been attempted. These daughters may have become mothers to some of us.

Researchers estimate that one in four pregnancies are not wanted, with many ending in termination, where that option is available

How wanted and welcomed into the world we were as a baby, varies greatly. If we were an 'accident' or the result of coercive sex; or were created to fulfil some need in our mother or her relationship with our father; or to meet the requirements or expectations of others, or even from an apathetic disregard for what happens, we are likely to be experienced as an unwelcome intrusion in the life of the mother, an emotion that is then transmitted to us.

We never really know the motivation for our mother conceiving and giving birth to us, unless she tells us and it becomes one of those family myths that we are required to carry, until we decide not to. We may know 'she had to get married' or *'her parents disowned her for being pregnant'* – situations that are now less likely in the modern world. Some mothers tell their daughters, *"Having you ruined my life"* or *"I had to give up everything for you"*, which indicates the depth of the resentment she holds. Other stories indicate a desire to save a relationship: *"Mum said she thought having a baby – me – would bring them together, and she was distraught when he left."*

Some women become mothers due to a romanticised idea about motherhood, rather than a deep desire to raise a child. Such a mother may think she wants a baby, but her heart or indeed her body may not be ready, in which case there can be a disconnect between what the daughter experiences in her mother's contact with her and what her mother says.

A daughter may notice that while her mother may have said she always wanted to be a mother and loved having children, her behaviour indicated something different in that she emotionally neglected the children. This disconnect can be incredibly confusing. Daughters in this situation are left feeling it is their fault for not being a lovable child, whilst continuing to try and prove how lovable she is throughout her life.

Some daughters are not wanted for themselves. For example, the family story may be that a daughter was born to replace a sister who had died; she may even be given her deceased sister's name as her middle name. She may carry this sense of being a replacement deep inside and for years be unable to want or love herself; her capacity for feeling self-worth had been badly damaged and in many ways she discounted herself. It is understandable that a mother may want another child. However, if grief has not been fully processed, the dead child and the new daughter can become merged in the mother's mind and in how she relates to the living daughter. The living daughter senses this disconnect, and it affects the loving connection between her and her mother. Her mother might also be more anxious with her new baby, fearing she too may die, and daughters may imbibe that anxiety as a young child.

Sometimes daughters are told they weren't really the 'right child', as their father only wanted a boy; the mother may tell the story of having to apologise for having another girl. As a result, the daughter won't feel welcomed or cherished and may internalise the message that they should have been someone else. They may well end up feeling responsible for things not feeling right, without knowing what they feel responsible for; their capacity for self-esteem will also be affected. They may try all their lives to be 'worthy of something' until they realise what is really going on. Eventually, in some cases, daughters will find their way to a deeper connection with themselves where this story no longer defines them or their behaviour.

Some mothers, driven by an inner experience that they are not conscious of, may see their daughter as an interloper, a perpetrator to whom the mother feels a victim. Such mothers say things like, *"I don't know what you want from me"* or *"Look how much I gave up for you"*; *"I could have been a successful dancer if you hadn't come along"* or *"You were a difficult baby and you took away my life."* In this way, the mother demonises the child. Such mothers carry a deeply hurt and vulnerable child within themselves, a hurt which is outside their conscious awareness, but which reverberates in her relationship with her daughter. As a way of coping, she sees in her baby what she can't bear to be in connection with in herself and may carry an unconscious desire to 'kill off the monster/daughter'. It is not the daughter's fault nor responsibility that her mother's history made it hard for her to want or love her child.

Those whose mothers are negative, critical, narcissistic (always self-centred) or controlling learn that they as their unique selves are not wanted. Such daughters are not allowed a life of their own where they can express themselves and make their own decisions. There is little space for them to expand into themselves. They are required to put limits on themselves, to discount parts of themselves and aspects of their experience – and of course, they take that into adulthood. For example, if as children we told our mother that we were scared about something, she may have responded, *"Don't be so stupid, you're not scared"* or maybe if we had hurt ourselves we hear, *"Don't make such a fuss, it doesn't hurt that much"*; or if we ask for a cuddle, our needs are discounted by the response, *"Oh, grow up will you – I haven't got time to waste."* I often observe this when I'm in a café or shop, watching parents discount or contradict a child. How confusing it is for a child to feel something and be told they don't.

On the other hand, it is wonderful at times to see young girls in, what to my eyes might seem eccentric, bright outfits, proud and energised at having chosen what they want to wear and being allowed to do that. They are often skipping and dancing with great smiles lighting their faces and it fills my heart to know there are mothers and parents who want to cherish their daughters' individuality. For many of us, we didn't have that degree of joyfulness in our lives, perhaps through poverty but mostly because our mothers wouldn't let us become 'ourselves', we needed to be an extension of her. Mothers who are controlling may repeatedly limit their daughters' ability to choose for themselves what they want to wear and do. A daughter's memory may be full of having to wear hated clothes and not allowed to do things.

The daughter of a narcissistic mother quickly learns that she doesn't really exist as her own person in her mother's eyes, and even as an adult, her life and work is likely to be ignored or discounted. Who she is, is of no interest to a narcissistic mother; she is not wanted for herself. Mothers can be very cruel, knowing how to hurt their daughter, and maybe then making a joke of it. Such mothers see others as an audience for her. The daughter often continues to try to be noticed by her mother but is repeatedly hurt. Narcissistic mothers can interpret anything they don't like about their daughter as being deliberately hurtful. The daughter may become dutiful as a way of managing the relationship while never getting any affirmation or sense of being liked for herself.

When I had finished rewriting this chapter and sat down with a cup of coffee to consider it, I had an overwhelming sense that I hadn't fully lived my own life either, despite no doubt appearing to from the outside. I could feel all the ways in which I had limited myself by my early programming. I became tearful and was on the edge of falling down the rabbit hole of self-pity, when I caught myself, and thought, *"Well I'm not dead yet so what does this mean for tomorrow, next week, and the time I have left?"* The opportunity to live differently is always there. My work as a psychotherapist, coach and author has been about choice and agency, that is, reclaiming ourselves from the grip of our childhood. At times I forget this for myself.

Being wanted at all, and being wanted for ourselves, are key to our fulfilment as people. If we didn't have the sensations of being wanted as a child, we carry that within us and may continue to limit ourselves in ways we don't need to, now we are adults. But for others to want us for ourselves, we have to want ourselves first and foremost, by which I mean we have to accept our validity as a person in our own right, with our own desires, needs and passions – which have nothing to do with what our mother wants of us. We must accept that we have a right to our own unique and wonderful life, irrespective of what anyone else thinks of us. We may have to put effort into this, but it enables us to turn around the impact of the past, so that we are no longer living in it. The first step is to recognise that not being wanted was not about us; this includes not being wanted for ourselves, for our childish vitality and developing character.

The opportunity to live differently is always there

Accepting ourselves for who we are and wanting to be that person is an integral part of loving ourselves unconditionally. We can explore how and in what ways we discount ourselves, our needs, our feelings, talents, body and experience. Remember, some of us were taught to do this as children, so we need to learn how to stop doing it now and put different responses in place. We can reflect on where any restrictions are in our lives that we have created, consciously or unconsciously. If we bring these into our conscious awareness, we then have choices, either to continue as we are, or to change.

Wanting ourselves means we no longer need to adapt to others, in ways that are not healthy for us. Of course, we have unconscious behaviour and unprocessed emotions which can negatively influence how we are with others, but we can learn about these constrictions and change them. Wanting ourselves is wanting whatever it is we need to live well and fully, with joy and a sense of inner freedom. Understanding this comes via a mixture of self-reflection and learning through being in relationship, which can be a therapeutic one or with a loving partner who wants us to become fully ourselves. As with all learning, it is a spiral, and gradual, but it is worth our attention.

Spiral of Learning

If you really want to experience yourself, in the fullness of your being, what three (or more) things would you do differently or additionally in the next 2 weeks? For example:

- *I'd value myself and what I do*
- *I would claim one thing I want for myself*
- *I'd see success in all I do, even things that don't go well as that is how I experiment and learn*

What one thing do you really want to do for yourself? Maybe it is to go on a painting, writing or spiritual retreat, or have a couple of days away in somewhere you'd love to be, or creating a whole day just for yourself without meeting the demands of anyone else.

Write a short story about a woman, who is the same age as you, who embodies wanting and loving herself:

What is her life like?

How does she organise her time and relationships?

What is she doing with her talents and resourcefulness?

How does she resource herself?

How does her light shine into her world?

CHAPTER 13
Protecting Yourself Now If You Weren't Protected Then

Some daughters had the experience of not being protected by those who were supposed to protect them, and were exposed to anger, cruelty, violence and sexual abuse. This may be as well as exposure to not feeling loved or wanted, and from other traumatising experiences. As children we were unable to protect ourselves from the harmful behaviour of those we lived with or who were part of our family or small community. The betrayal of our trust in those we looked to for our safety and wellbeing leaves a deep legacy. The memory pathways may be highly sensitive to being activated in the here and now, including in our relationship with our mother. As adults, we can reclaim and protect ourselves through therapeutic processing of our experience.

How does it feel not to be protected from harm as a child? It is terrifying, as we are powerless and there is nowhere we can go for our safety. We are traumatised by the cruelty of whoever enacts it, whether in the home or in a trusted community, religious institutions or schools. The space where it happens no longer feels like a safe haven, but a place where we have to be on our guard. This is particularly acute when it is our home. We become hyper-vigilant and fearful, like a meerkat, looking for signs of the next aerial invasion from an eagle or land ambush from a fox. Even so, these shocks may arrive unpredictably despite our vigilance. As it is so hard to acknowledge that those who are supposed to love and protect us, instead do us harm, we can start to attack ourselves, self-blaming and maybe self-harming.

The experience of many daughters is that of having cruel, self-interested, or addicted mothers. Such mothers are unpredictable, and it can be like constantly walking on egg shells. It is terrifying and the daughter is likely to keep her head down and try to be invisible. She may grow up hating confrontation and finding it hard to be assertive.

Most mothers deny the impact of their anger or violence, some may want the daughter to collude with a story about how forgiving or how tolerant the daughter was, ignoring the terror that had been caused. If such a daughter is entangled, she may take it as a compliment and go along with it, before realising how it really felt to be invited to join an illusion. Protecting ourselves is to honour our experience and not to collude with such a mother.

The angry outbursts and cruel behaviour are rarely talked about and are carried silently by mother and daughter making a healthy relationship impossible. It can be hard to raise the topic as the mother is likely to put up many defences as in the examples above. It's not impossible and it may be that a mother is willing to talk about what had been going on for her. We all need to realise that anger and violence directed at us, isn't about us, it is about the mother.

For other daughters it was their father's or step-father's violence that terrified them, and their mother who unable to provide protection, because she herself was terrified. Too often, those who might have stepped in fail to do so. It is sadly too often the case that no one outside the family appeared to notice the bruising or took appropriate preventative action if they were told about the violence. Children in such cases can feel abandoned by all who should protect them. Perhaps for some daughters with abusive mothers, their father stepped in to stop the abuse but often it occurs when the father wasn't in the home. Fathers or mothers will often feel deep shame, when from their terror of their own partner, they are unable to protect their children. Everyone keeps silent as it is too painful and shaming to talk about.

Sometimes, if the father is angry and violent, a mother, terrified of being hit if she said anything, may try to recruit a daughter to try to calm Dad down. She may ask the child to learn how to pacify the father. From a young age, the daughter can take on feeling responsible for saving the family. It is distressing for the child to see how vulnerable their mother was, and to see her being hit. Children in a family with a violent father may respond differently, one daughter may develop hatred for her father while her sister or brother may side with him and see mother as the problem. A daughter may try to become 'daddy's little girl' as a way of protecting herself having witnessed that her mother couldn't protect her.

Children can feel responsible from a young age that they must become the family saviour

All these daughters are trapped by this domestic violence. In too many cases, neither the father nor the mother was able to protect the daughter from violence in the home; nor did the wider family or close community step in. We know that too often women are disbelieved when they speak up about domestic violence or are blamed – so many don't report it and suffer in silence. They often have nowhere to go and no means to support themselves, and so become trapped and powerless. They are overwhelmed by the power of the violence. This can be equally true of men subject to the violence of women.

All who inflict harm on others had harm inflicted on them. It is not an inevitable consequence of children who are abused that they abuse others, but a history of abuse is always present in those who are violent. They are acting out from the 'there and then' of their own experience as they have never learnt how to control their rage or impulses. Their behaviour leaves a deep legacy of fear, terror and a lack of safety. As a result, many daughters learn not to upset people who are angry and unpredictable, while burying the anger and rage they feel. They are likely to monitor those around them for signs of any eruption and find it hard to relax in some settings. They may find it very hard to be around confrontation or anger of any kind.

All who inflict harm on others had harm inflicted on them

While domestic abuse is usually obvious within the household, if not outside, sexual abuse is often hidden in the home, or close community, as well as to outsiders. Not only is home no longer a place of safety, it houses a secret shared by the perpetrator and the one who is being abused. This makes it potentially highly toxic to our emotional wellbeing. The demand to keep sexual abuse a secret adds a huge burden on the child. It is common for the perpetrator to tell the child they mustn't tell anyone or something bad will happen to them, for example, that they will be taken away. This plants a deep fear of being found out and the terror of the consequences that may result, and so the secret may be held for years and years. This makes it impossible for the emotional impact to be processed and for the victim to find release from the straight jacket they have been placed in.

Being sexually abused by those to whom we turn to for love and comfort, or who is a brother or step-brother and who we should be able to trust, is a betrayal. It is devastating to be betrayed in this way and there is no escape. In many situations an abused daughter's mother either never knew or did know and kept silent about it. Most daughters never tell her about it, so never found out whether her mother knew about the abuse or not. In this way, daughters can feel betrayed by both parents. Understandably, such daughters lose an emotional connection with her mother and father because of the abuse. She and her siblings suffered it alone.

The typical pattern is one of 'having to keep the secret', of feeling shame and betrayal, rage and fear, at the same time, often thinking (correctly or not) that we would not be believed if we speak up, coupled with the fear that it is already known of, and still no one bothers to protect us. Unfortunately, too often children who did speak up were not believed and were blamed for making up terrible stories about their parents. We can witness this in the cases of children who were sexually abused in religious schools or children's homes, and who were silenced for years. The situation seems to be slowly easing for today's children, perhaps because in our more open society, there is greater awareness of sexual abuse and its lasting legacy, and so there is more help, support and sensitive care for children to speak up and be believed, whatever the consequences for the family system.

The enactor of harm rarely accepts the reality and impact of their actions. How they survive their shame is through denial and illusion and by getting others to collude with them that they are good people or that those they abused deserved or wanted it. They survive by blaming the victim. Victim blaming can be very confusing for a child. Often the child is told she was the cause of the violence, or she wanted the sex or seduced the abuser. The perpetrator's denial often includes that it didn't do the child any harm and that it was a form of 'love'. It wasn't and it never is. Victim blaming allows the abuser to stay in denial so they never have to face the reality.

Victim blaming can also be part of how some non-violent, but demanding mothers manage their relationship with their daughter. Where the mother is narcissistic, she may feel that she is the victim of the child's wilfulness or individuality and sees the daughter as being the perpetrator, intentionally wanting to hurt her, the mother. This is a reversal of what is the case as in reality, the mother is the perpetrator, and her daughter is the victim. As a result, the daughter often grows up thinking everything is her fault; that she isn't a good enough daughter, that she failed in some ways and her mother suffered as a result. The perpetrator and victim are not correctly identified. This continues into adult life, until we understand the distortion that we have been caught up in.

We can become aware of how we may have been blamed for something that we were the victim of. This is part of protecting ourselves. When we recognise this, we can refuse to accept the blame attributed to us. We are not responsible for the behaviour of others. Women are often blamed for what happens to them, so this distortion is a mirror of what occurs often in society.

Victim blaming allows the abuser to stay in denial, so they never have to face the reality

Those who abuse others and are in denial rarely take responsibility for their actions, if it is spoken about it can be an invitation to collude with a sanitised version of events or to be relieved of their responsibility. Stepping out of denial would require something to be said like *"I am so sorry that I hit you. I was finding life very difficult, but I shouldn't have taken it out on you. It was wrong and I know you were deeply hurt by what I did"*. A truthful response from an abused daughter might be *"yes you hurt me often, I didn't feel safe and had no one to turn to. I was terrified of you"*. We need to be careful of longing for a real acknowledgement of the pain caused as it can keep us stuck. We know the pain caused to us and its legacy, we have lived with it for a long time and we can heal from it without our parent taking responsibility.

One of the consequences of being abused by someone who is supposed to love us and who we love, is that we can grow up confusing love and abuse. This can mean that we don't recognise people who might do us harm, or if we do, we may think loving them enough will change them. This is why some who have been abused enter into abusive relationships as adults or end up working for narcissists or bullies. We are seeking love and respect in the wrong place. We can believe 'we understand them' or 'can save them' and the dynamic is so familiar that in a distorted way, it feels 'normal'.

Conversely, we may have highly attuned antennae for abusers, or see potential abuse in all we are close to, finding it difficult to trust anyone and we develop many defences to keep people away from us, particularly those who want to get close. Some daughters notice that they may try to harm those they are in a relationship with or be cruel. If we have been unable to process our experience we may 'act out' towards others, speaking harshly or critically to and about others, undermining others, and bullying others either through anger outbursts or even physical attack.

When we berate or attack ourselves, do ourselves harm or put ourselves in dangerous situations, part of us is enacting the abuser. We become a victim to ourselves and continue what the parent started. Those of us who may have had difficulties with food in the past were trying to find a way of surviving our internal distress but through harming ourselves. Overworking is also harmful to us as we ignore our exhaustion, it is a betrayal of ourselves. We can raise our awareness of the ways in which we may be doing ourselves harm, rather than wanting and loving ourselves with compassion.

The helplessness we felt as children can be activated when we feel overwhelmed in the 'here and now'. This helplessness may also lead us to old thoughts from childhood that no one loves us or wants us, and everyone is against us. This brings a collapse of our sense of agency, that is our capacity to direct our own lives healthily, in circumstances where we can act for ourselves and are not being an actual victim of perpetration. We may look for a rescuer who we hope may save us from this overwhelm. Of course, when we were a victim, no rescuer came, but now we are adults, we can rescue ourselves and looking for a rescuer serves only to invite co-dependency and entanglement. I make this sound simple, and I know for myself how hard it can be to sit with this sense of helplessness and collapse.

Looking for a rescuer serves only to invite co-dependency and entanglement

Being a victim of emotional, domestic or sexual abuse creates trauma wounds which only heal when we are able to process our experience. Until that time, we cover up the wounds with sticking plaster, but the 'bleeding' keeps seeping through and as for a physical wound, we hold ourselves stiffly so as not to reopen the wounds. Part of this may include trying to hide the wound from others as it is too painful to talk of, and we fear being overwhelmed by the shame. Processing the impact of emotional trauma on us heals the wound from the inside out, but such processing takes time and is a journey unique to each of us, and we may need therapeutic help to heal the wounds left.

Protecting ourselves requires honest self-reflection about our behaviour towards ourselves and others, together with a capacity to face the reality of our experience. It means challenging ourselves when we realise we are feeling responsible for the behaviour of others in the past and present. It means reviewing the boundaries we have in place with those who have abused us – if we are still in contact with them. This includes protecting ourselves from our mother's ongoing abuse, for example, we can learn to say 'no' and mean it, or *"I am not going to listen to you talking to me that way,"* or *"I don't like it when you continue to discount my family, (work/ achievements)."* We can put markers down for what is okay for us and what isn't. We will have to challenge the beliefs that have stopped us doing this before, so that we can change the patterns of old. Making any kind of change takes courage as it challenges our fears of abandonment and of not being loved or protected. We can also protect ourselves by not expecting our mother to change and by not picking up her invitation to be a victim to her behaviour, by feeling responsible or that we have to rescue her. It also requires us notice when we are being cruel, unkind and unloving to ourselves or being an abuser to others, and to take stock and change such thoughts or behaviour. These are all ways we can start to move out of the tangled web.

Spiral of Learning

Not being protected leaves us in a vulnerable position and trusting others can become hard. Reading about such abuse that you might have also encountered can stimulate challenging feelings. If that is the case, please do something that is resourcing for you. What is the most valuable thing you could do for yourself and shows that you are protecting yourself?

Bring to mind some examples in the present of how you are protecting yourself. It may help to write about these and recognise all that you are doing. What inner resources are you accessing?

How might you use these inner resources in situations where maybe you are not protecting yourself as lovingly as you might? Are there additional internal resources that you may need to access? For example, self-belief, confidence, walking away or asking for support in doing that?

It can really help to talk to someone we trust about our experiences of domestic and/or sexual abuse, and to have our experience witnessed and felt by the other person, without judgement. Talking helps release the knots that have been created in our relationship web and within ourselves.

CHAPTER 14
How We Survived

In the previous chapters I talked of how we adapt emotionally and psychologically, enabling us to continue living in circumstances that cause emotional trauma. All causes of trauma, including distressing life events, result in our danger response being activated to an intense level and overwhelmed. This creates a 'trauma state' within us, which is the tangled knotted web I describe. This web has many different elements that affect our behaviour, beliefs, and emotions, and they in turn influence our responses in the present, long after they originated – and for as long as we continue not to pay attention to them through self-reflection and, for some, therapy.

The good thing to know is that we can all become more self-aware in the present, rather than driven by the past. If you have been doing some of the exercises in the book so far, you have been using your capacity to do that; looking at yourself, observing and sensing yourself, hopefully with compassion and curiosity. In this way, we learn how to listen closely to ourselves, beyond the surface chatter and defences we put in place. We can attend to ourselves no matter how big or knotted our trauma state is, and we all retain this capacity. Attending to ourselves may need practice, but the more we do it, the stronger we become. As this happens, the more able we are to notice how our negative self-talk, self-criticism and distorted beliefs try to step in and take over, just like our mother or parents might have done when we were children, limiting our emergence as an individual. We will also notice how self-pity can well up and distract us from learning about ourselves. Maybe that happened in childhood when our mother or main carer, used her self-pity to dampen us down. It might arise from a desire to get acknowledgement and comfort, which it rarely provides, it just takes us into misery and perhaps overwhelm.

Therapists working in the field of emotional trauma name this capacity to observe and sense ourselves as our 'Healthy Self', our 'I' or the 'Self'. These are resources within us for our capacity to love, want and be able to protect ourselves, to be compassionate to ourselves and others, to be curious and creative. It is a wonderful resource to develop, and we all have access to it. It can be diminished by trauma dynamics, but these resources are always there, ready and waiting for us to revive them. We can be supported in developing them through our own practice of reflection, working with a therapist or through other personal or spiritual development and growth processes. As with all trauma healing, it is 'work in progress' and is rarely instantaneous.

As we saw earlier in this book, we find myriad ways to survive our childhoods when they are not loving and holding. These survival behaviours were our life saviours. I have heard them referred to as our 'childhood heroes'. I like that term as it is too easy to see survival states as negative and wrong. As we move into adulthood however, they no longer serve us well, becoming maladaptive and bringing problems into our lives. Working with them requires compassion for our younger self, who needed to find a way to stay in relationship with her mother and father.

Survival behaviours were our life saviours

Our internal trauma state has different components. At the deepest level are the emotions from the time of response of being overwhelmed – these include rage, terror, shame, vulnerability, hurt and a painful sense of our aloneness. While we bury these deep within us, in our unconscious, we experience them when they are activated in the 'here and now'. As an example, sometimes I feel an aching loneliness, which is nothing to do with being around people or not but is buried deep inside childhood and grief; my 'grieving child'. This can easily morph into the 'self-pitying' survival part of me, but over time I have learnt how to give this grief some space without doing that. I have to engage my self-compassion so I am better able to witness my grief, rather than being all-consumed by it or berate myself for feeling it. Through reflecting on our responses to situations in the present we can bring them more into our conscious awareness where we can recognise them with compassion. We can sometimes identify these as our 'wounded child', 'hurt child', 'betrayed, lost or emotionally abandoned child' or whatever resonates most with you. They are held within us at the age at which they occurred. We may have several layers of them, relating to our traumatising experience, for example, the three year old, six year old, nine year old and so on.

We develop ways to survive these deep emotions so we can

continue to stay attached to our parents in any way we can and keep living. Professor Ruppert (2014) calls this aspect of our internalised trauma dynamics our Survival Self. To help our understanding of what this may involve I have identified four groups:

- *Freezing, numbness and dissociation: how we protected ourselves at the time of the overwhelming experience.*
- *Denial, illusion, ways we block any knowledge of our trauma state and history*
- *Adaptive patterns of behaviour, thoughts and feeling that have become habitual. These include the ways we adapted as children to the mothering and parenting we received; others are ways we have found to survive our experience*
- *Negative self-talk, self-beliefs and adapted identity: a survival sense of who we are, taken from, and adapted to, those around us.*

We can change all of these if we bring them into our awareness, connect with and process the sensations and emotions they are trying to protect.

I have to engage my self-compassion so I am better able to witness my grief, rather than being all-consumed by it

The three trauma symptoms of freezing, numbness, and dissociation are associated with how our neuro-physiology responded to our overwhelming experience. Emotions may become frozen and numb, this can show up when people are in close personal relationships, including mothers who may find it hard to emotionally connect with their daughters. Numbness is a way of bearing our emotional pain. We may meet this in writing in the reflective journal and asking 'what do I feel' and the answer being 'nothing'. We can just note that and be curious. We needn't berate ourselves but compassionately recognise this is a way of protecting ourselves. We can learn how to unfreeze and un-numb our feelings, the starting point is to recognise we have frozen and numb parts within us. We may continue to try to numb ourselves emotionally through addictions of all kinds including through work, drugs, alcohol, gambling, sex or shopping

We have met the survival states of denial and illusion in the last chapter. These are ways we blank out what is too painful to accept; or ways in which we create a different version of events to avoid the truth or involve magical thinking. I have met strong denial in myself twice in my life concerning serious health issues. While part of me did know my life was in danger, I simultaneously refused to believe it. It was very powerful learning about how strongly denial operated within me, and I have since experienced other situations where I have noted this denial, now I am aware of it. This is an example of how a trauma state involves a split within our psyche so that we are not operating as an integrated whole; part of us knows, part of us denies knowing. The part that knows is connected to our implicit memory, the part that denies is from our survival desire to hide from the truth.

A trauma state involves a split within our psyche so that we are not operating as an integrated whole

We also survive in situations of intense stress through a response called dissociation. which means we shut down the information pathways from our body and hide behind a mask. We might feel disconnected, not really present, vague, or just going through the motions, as if we have switched ourselves off. This will be a response to something in the other person or setting that has activated the fear response of the past. It might be not being seen, or a raised voice or having our experience dismissed. When we 'come back to ourselves' we may feel very upset. We learnt how to dissociate as children and, we may find we do this at times when with our mother or in conversation with her. We can feel we 'have left the room' and the mask we leave goes into automatic pilot mode. It helps us shut out the anger or pain and is a powerful way of managing the contact in the moment. However, we might want to ask ourselves *"What would help me not to deploy this strategy more than is good for me?'* and consider how to process the anger and pain differently.

Defending ourselves from reality can help us survive, especially as children when we can't go anywhere else. As adults, some daughters continue with a form of denial that includes saying things like, *"It was nothing much"*, or *"Well, we all have our crosses to bear"*, or *"Compared to others it was nothing."* Of course, we might not always want to talk honestly about our experiences with some people, but we do need to be honest with ourselves if we are to move beyond our history. It was never *'nothing'* it was more often like, *'so much it overwhelmed me.'* Comparisons with others is unhelpful as it can lead us to diminish our own felt experience as a child. Clinging to the idea that we had a happy childhood, when we didn't – for whatever reason – is both denial of reality and an illusion. We are creating a fantasy for ourselves that ultimately prevents us from processing our experience.

If the person we looked to for unconditional love is unable to give it to us, or harms us, we use our adapted child survival strategies to try to appease her or get close to her in the hope it will change things; this is unlikely to work. Unfortunately, we often keep these strategies going into adulthood with our mother and with others we are in a relationship with. Many of these strategies we have met before including the rescuer; the parent to the parent; the one, or part (a bundle of thoughts, emotions and behaviour), who feels responsible for everything; the entangled caretaker; the one who clings to others; the heroic saviour; and the one who keeps an untrusting distance from people. Because these are well formed habitual responses, they form part of our reaction before we have even noticed. However, with practice, we can catch ourselves before we react, we can step back, and then decide how we want to respond instead. We can notice these reactive patterns and name them in ways that have meaning for us – *"Ah, I recognise here that my 'rescuer' is trying to make peace with my mother."* In this way, we can become better at recognising when these are still acting unhelpfully in our lives.

Other knots in the web are formed by bundles of habitual thinking, emotions and behaviour, developed to manage our relationships. Narcissism, negativity, the 'martyr', the 'control-freak', are all examples of these and are mobilised to keep people at a distance, as emotional closeness feels too dangerous to the 'wounded child'. The fear of being hurt is too much. We have also met the 'perpetrator' and the 'self-pitying part' in the previous chapter; these too, keep people at a distance, for the same reason.

Another aspect of our self maybe the 'addict', who may use work, sex, food, drink, drugs, exercise, or shopping as a way to bear the pain or control the anger. Addictions give us an immediate high, but we need more and more of a fix to keep getting temporary satisfaction. Many daughters talk of using over-work, or 'work addiction', as a way of surviving; they bury themselves in their work and the demands that go with it. This leaves no space for self-reflection and joy, or for the healthy resources to grow. It can also be a desperate attempt to be noticed and acknowledged and to avoid being abandoned or fired. We may also have parts that could be named the 'over-achiever' or the 'perfectionist' – these too are ways in which we try to keep ourselves safe. Unfortunately, while all these strategies might initially deliver useful outcomes such as income and status, they often lead to ill health and can end in burnout.

Some people use their 'joker' self to put a distance between their inner feelings and other people. They might have learnt that joking or clowning offered a distraction to the family from any tensions that existed, or it was used to hide behind, like a mask. It offered a way to pretend that everything was 'all right'. In my experience, such an adaptive survival strategy is more common in men, but I recall for myself 'being the entertainer' as a child, and even now I sometimes hear myself using a 'jokey' response to things, at times inappropriately and self-deprecatingly. Of course, humour is a wonderful diffuser of tension and we can use it skilfully in our interactions with our mother and others; but that is not the same as having this 'joker' part that comes from a place of emotional pain. When I use its healthy version, it diffuses a pattern of responding.

Other common survival strategies include control which can show itself as managing or planning or 'taking over' as well as wanting to control the behaviour and life choices of others and of herself. If a daughter grew up in a chaotic family, with a mother who was inconsistent, she may become the 'family manager or organiser' as a way of trying to restore some order into her life. Whatever type of family or parenting we had, if it brought anxiety we may develop controlling-type strategies to manage our internal state. My version is 'planning', an attempt to control the future. I see this as growing out of the shock and confusion of my father's death. When I feel internal agitation, I get on the internet, booking and organising the future. All such strategies are driven by an underlying anxiety about abandonment, safety, being wanted and loved. Most of our survival strategies have a positive side, being able to manage, organise, and plan are useful skills. Like controlling ourselves and others as an attempt to manage reality, these survival strategies take on a driven quality to the extent that they can also exhaust us and do not lead to healthy relationships. The developmental challenge is to keep the healthy resources these strategies provide, while letting go of the survival mechanisms through understanding what lies beneath them. Knowing the difference is key.

Observing our Adapted Selves

In self-reflection we meet these adapted parts of ourselves. We may then start berating ourselves for their presence, which doesn't help. Instead, to paraphrase Dr Richard Swartz, we should welcome all parts, and the feelings that go with them, no matter how apparently dysfunctional they are in our lives as adults. This might involve thinking something like, *"Here you are again, welcome. Thank you for helping me survive for all this time, but I can take over now."* That might sound a bit 'woo-woo' or weird for some, but it is better than attacking ourselves for an emotion or for activating a pattern or pretending that it doesn't exist. In this way, by welcoming the adapted parts of ourselves, we are recognising rather than denying that something made us act this way. To free ourselves from the tangled, knotted web we need to break the patterns by becoming aware of them, understanding them and reminding ourselves that we are now resourceful adults and we can make decisions and take action.

Some beliefs and thoughts that are also survival patterns are those of self-criticism, self-punishment, low self-esteem and low self-belief, and perhaps self-hatred. We may also have internalised messages about who we are that we have come to live by, but when we examine these, we realise we are not like that and that accepting them was all part of developing a survival identity. This is where wanting, loving and protecting ourselves is important. We now know that these survival patterns and beliefs come from the 'there and then'; they are not based on objective reality, but a view we have internalised from others or their behaviour towards us or told ourselves. Turning this around and relinquishing these beliefs can be challenging but catching them when they are present and identifying their impact is a good place to start. At some level, they are all likely to have been formed in an attempt to keep ourselves safe, and to avoid punishment and abandonment.

If we take this self-awareness and understanding about our inner trauma state and our relationship with our mother (or father/ other care-giver), we can see how our different tangled webs may be knotted together. We can move beyond this entanglement, but we can't change how our mother has learnt to survive, and it is not our responsibility to rescue her from that. However, we can change how we have survived by reducing the size of the tangled trauma web within and create more space and energy for the life we truly want to live.

This is exactly what many daughters work towards. We may have been repeatedly tripped up by our mother, falling into the same old patterns with her and feeling helpless to change how we relate to her and the feelings the interactions leave us with. Some may recognise that they have developed relational skills in work settings where they manage some demanding and challenging relationships. If we have these skills, we can transfer them to relating to our mother, and may be delighted to see how well they work. When we change our responses, our mother will not like it and may try harder to get us back to the old patterns but with renewed confidence we can avoid that invitation.

We can move beyond this entanglement, but we can't change how our mother has learnt to survive, and it is not our responsibility to rescue her from that

We can develop our self-awareness of the patterns and engage with the feelings we have. From our healthy resources, we can see a way forward and put that into action. Our 'there and then' was no longer in the driving seat.

Most trauma therapists recognise that many mental and physical illnesses (for example, auto-immune diseases) are also trauma symptoms. All our physiological body systems, including the immune and endocrine systems, are affected by the trauma response. Some talk of trauma being 'held in the body', and the body 'remembers', for that reason. Mental illnesses are seen by many as ways that we have evolved to manage our pain and distress. I haven't gone into detail about such illness here as it is a topic for other books, nonetheless, emotional trauma and mental health are inextricably linked. Some daughters have talked about mothers with mental illness and alcoholism and the impact this had on their childhood. In many such situations, looking at the mother's own childhood history gives an indicator of the trauma she is suffering. If we suffer from depression, anxiety, anorexia, or bipolar disorder ourselves, it can help immensely to seek out skilled professional help to enable us to move beyond these patterns or to manage what we can't leave behind in the best ways we can.

The quality of the relationship we have with our body is affected by emotional or physical trauma shocks to our system. The trauma response protects us by disrupting the information that travels from the body to the brain, and thus blocks emotions from arising. This can make it hard for some to feel into their body. They are not able to say, *"I feel agitation in my gut"*, or *"I feel a numbness in my arm"* or *"an emptiness here (pointing to a part of the body)"*; or if asked, where they feel anger or sadness in their body, they are unable to say. Not being able to feel our emotional trauma can affect the quality of our self-awareness, but the good news is we can develop our awareness over time and with practice.

To recap, we managed to survive through the amazing responses of our bodies and minds. The internalised trauma dynamic is made up of the feelings stored at the times of the overwhelm to our neuro-physiology, which we try to push well out of our conscious awareness but which continue to influence us in the here and how. It also involves the survival responses, survival behaviour and thinking patterns we created to keep attached to our care-givers and to try to understand our experience. It is these which entangle us with our mother, and her with us.

Spiral of Learning

What have you noticed that has resonated with you in this chapter? What has particularly stood out for you? What, if anything, has disturbed you? If anything has been disturbing, as before, please do something that is resourcing for yourself and come back to these spiral of change suggestions another time. This is expressing love for yourself.

What activities or experiences feel nurturing for you? List three or four. Pick two and decide how to bring more of them into your life right now, not in a few weeks time, but from this point forward.

As part of your self-reflection note down any survival strategy habits you notice, for example managing, organising, controlling, denial, magical thinking (illusion), dissociation, or addictions, how they operate in your life, and with your mother particularly. Use your curiosity and self-compassion, so that you can reflect on them without judgement. Just notice and observe them, as if you are a third-party.

If at any time you feel overwhelmed, take a 'step back', focus on your breathing and remind yourself that (a) you have survived, and (b) that you can find a way to move beyond this trauma state. Remember that many of us need a good therapist to work with at times in our lives to help us find healing through processing our experience. Doing this is an expression of our love and care for ourselves, of investing in our wellbeing.

If you want to know more about the full impact of emotional trauma, I have included some books in the Bibliography. Read them, go to workshops, look online, educate yourself and deepen your understanding. My learning about the impact of emotional trauma has come from the skilled work and teaching of Professor Franz Ruppert, Dr Richard Swartz, Dr Gabor Maté, Thomas Hübl, Dr Stephen Porges, Dr Daniela Sieff, Marion Woodman, Alice Miller and Dr Bessel van der Kolk. There are YouTube clips of many of these practitioners talking about trauma and their work.

CHAPTER 15
Russian Dolls: Grandmother, Mother and You

'I live now in a house that is one corner of a triangle. At one of the other corners is the home my mother had for thirty years and died in. At the third corner is the last home of my grandmother, where she also died. These homes are all within 8 minutes' walk of each other. I see this as a symbol in some way of how we are entangled or connected, I can't decide which. My grandmother grew up in what is now one of the shops in our small high street, where in later years, my mother had her hair done. I wasn't close to my grandmother, but I have learnt over the years what a negative impact she had on my mother. Why have we all ended up here? Were we all searching for the same thing?

I was listening to a Buddhist teacher recently who said, "We are all searching for loving kindness." That rang true. His point was that we look for it externally rather than internally. But I wonder if all three of us were looking for some loving kindness and maternal holding and found something in the sea and countryside where we ended up?'
– Personal reflection

As I mentioned in the earlier parts of this book, for all women, 'my grandmother, mother and me' are nested together like Russian Dolls. In many cases, our grandmother's earliest experiences will have resulted in the internalisation of emotional trauma, creating a wounded, hurt, betrayed or abandoned child who had to find her own ways to survive as a child. She will then have mothered our mother, without having processed her wounds, and so is likely to unwittingly engender more wounds in her daughter. This is how emotional trauma is passed on through the generations. If despite these challenges, our mother has a well-developed and mature healthy Self, then a loving connection will have resulted with her own daughters; if she didn't, then we will experience a broken or disturbed connection involving distorted love. All of us have the capacity to pass on healthy resources, even if we are traumatised, including the ability to keep going with a life, and to create loving relationships is also transgenerational.

Understanding emotional trauma and its legacy can help broaden our perspective of the ancestral element of our trauma and help us see our mother more fully in her own history. We can understand that this didn't start with us, rather that we emerge from a long line of women, one nested within another, who have all suffered – some considerably – within their own families and in relation to external circumstances including war, racism and ethnic purges. All these women found a way to survive, to give birth to a daughter and in many cases also to raise that daughter. Knowing this can help us step back from any drama we have with our mother and place it in a wider context.

The passing on of emotional trauma isn't inevitable and we can diminish the intensity of the transmission through developing our own self-awareness and healing work. In previous generations, there were few opportunities for education, psychotherapy or trauma healing processes; no one understood how damaging the dynamics were. Every generation of women has been affected by the societal expectations and demands. Think how quickly circumstances can change depending on the government in a country or how communities become vilified due to changing attitudes and mores. Through reflective practice and developing conscious awareness of their patterns and habitual responses, women can change how their trauma state presents in their lives. However, where this hasn't happened, aspects of parenting most likely came from the survival parts of her mother and/or father, as they were caught in the circumstances of the time. To develop a sense of context, we may need to find out more about our parents' early lives, if they are still alive to share those stories.

Many mothers may have witnessed angry outbursts from both or either parent and sat on the stairs, or hidden, feeling scared and anxious. Some may have had a father who disappeared for times with the uncertainty of where he was and whether he was coming back again, this time. Maybe our mother had to fend for herself from an early age. Such mothers may become controlling as adults or because they had had to numb or freeze their emotions, they feel emotionally distant and can't talk about feelings.

Our grandmother may not have been able to be emotionally close to our mother, her own history of perhaps emotional abandonment, physical or sexual abuse, life experiences including war, and perhaps early loss of her mother or father. For many of our grandmothers and perhaps mothers, they grew up at a time when there wasn't any awareness that such experiences had a lasting impact on young children. It was 'your lot' and you just got on with it.

Many of our mothers may have been born into families where life was hard, and their mothers were worn down by childbirth and the practical demands of living, or where the rules of a religious or political regime limited women's rights and freedoms. Our mother might have escaped in her adolescence to another country or through pregnancy. We can imagine that our grandmothers were surviving and raising their families as best they could but couldn't protect their daughter from the demands of their situation nor were they able to create and sustain loving bonds with their daughters – life was too hard for that. We can imagine what life might have been like for the grandmother with no independence, no control over her own fertility, no help and little education. She did, however, raise a daughter, who raised a daughter who is now in the world and can take emotional responsibility for herself and bring good things to those around her.

The impacts of poor healthcare during pregnancy, childbirth and later childcare, were all common occurrences just a generation or two ago. Grandmothers died in childbirth, grandfathers might have died young, and babies died at birth or in infancy. There was little help or support for anyone with a disability, who had a mental illness, or was neuro-diverse, other than admission to a large hospital. Post-natal depression often went unrecognised, and mothers struggled through the early months of their babies' lives. Most families were left to cope alone. Those who lost their mother were often brought up by step-mothers, or relatives, who often did not want the added burden of the child of another. We can understand why our mothers' experience of being mothered may have been very poor, and why they may have become angry, negative or controlling mothers, they were caught in a tangled web of survival and possibly operating at the end of their resources for most of their life. Both mother and daughter become caught up in a dark web of transgenerational emotional trauma like Russian Dolls, one inside another.

Sharing stories of violence and anger in the home is more common, although may also be kept secret, along with other family history that brings shame with it. Our mothers may have experienced physical or sexual abuse and never told us. If she has, we can come to understand the lasting impact on her and how that shows itself in her behaviour.

Even where there isn't abuse, there are still many reasons for a child to carry emotional trauma. In addition to her relationship with her mother and father and her own distressing life events, she might have been caught in a war with the fear and uncertainty that brings; she might be the child of parents who were persecuted or even killed by a political regime; she might come from a long line of ancestors who have suffered racial abuse and segregation; she might have been subjected to poverty and hardship. Whatever we have experienced in our lives, our mother will have had her own version of it. We may think our experience is unique, and in some ways it is, however, we share aspects of it with our mothers, grandmothers and those before them. We are affected both by the relationship we have with our mother/parents, through their parenting from trauma and from the collective trauma they shared with others in relation to the societal context in which they were raised and lived.

Whatever we have experienced in our lives, our mother will have had her own version of it

Women are often blamed for things that are done to them and their stories are disbelieved. As they were so often financially dependent on men, if their relationship is abusive, they are likely to have nowhere else to go and so many suffer in silence. When I first got a mortgage, I had to have a guarantee for it from a man – my uncle – as I wasn't married but needed a male signatory. My mother, who'd had a mortgage for years, was not thought to be a suitable signatory, being female. It was only from 2021 that the mother's name will be on the marriage certificate of her daughter. For generations women have carried much stress and been unable to determine their own lives. They have been confined by societal restrictions on them and by the disparity between men and women around domestic tasks and child rearing. Our ancestors have all done their best to raise their daughters often within severe limitations, that is, limits to their own expectations, limits to the true expression of their personalities and desires and limited too by circumstance.

It is worth reiterating that whilst the experiences and fate of our father and our male ancestors are equally important to us as that of our mother (and undoubtedly, it helps us to find out more about that), I am focusing within this book on the female line. Most of us can go back in history to our grandparents, and some to great-grandparents. My grandparents were in their seventies when I was born, and I knew them for less than 8 years. My niece's children knew their great-grandmother (my mother) quite well, for fifteen years. For woman like me, the difference between my grandmother's and mother's childhoods and that of childhoods today is huge; whereas the children born to young mothers today may experience more similar cultural values although without doubt, these are ever-changing, especially with the impact of technology. While much has changed and continues to change, what doesn't change is the impact of abuse, racism, misogyny and not feeling wanted, loved or being protected.

Taking these considerations on board can help us gain a different perspective of our mother, especially if we can develop compassion for her early experiences and the nature of her own relationships with her mother and her father. We can honour the reality of our mother's experience and use it to shed some light on our experience of her. Once we understand that our mothers were locked into their own suffering and managing the best they could, we can perhaps empathise with why they failed their daughters through their action or inaction: because no doubt, they too had been failed. If they could have wanted, loved and protected us better, they would have done. If they had been wanted, loved and protected themselves, they would have been better equipped in their mothering. However, we must remember that it is not our fault or our responsibility that they were unable to do this. Our responsibility is to look to ourselves now we are adults and to examine our behaviour, actions and inactions, and decide if we are caught up in the past playing out in the present. If we are, then we have the opportunity to redefine our actions. The solutions to any relationship problems we have, with ourselves or with others, are not to be found in the lives of those who are now dead – their life events can shed light on our own, but their experience does not determine our lives. Only we can take responsibility for that.

Our responsibility is to look to ourselves now we are adults and to examine our behaviour, actions and inactions, and decide if we are caught up in the past playing out in the present

Spiral of Learning

Family Stories

What do you know about your grandmothers' and grandfathers' lives before they had children and the context in which they created a family? What stories have been handed down?

What do you know about your mother's childhood? Is it only from her or have aunts, uncles or cousins shared things that your mother hasn't?

Have you become aware of any secrets that have emerged but were unknown to your grandparents or mother when children?

You may want to write up their stories. You could do that as if they were writing them like a memoir or as if you were writing a novel.

CHAPTER 16
Supporting Learning and Change

Change comes from learning. Learning about ourselves comes from self-reflection and observation of our responses to those around us and to our life decisions. Bringing feelings and thoughts from our unconscious and making them conscious gives us more choices about how we want to behave and respond in the future.

This book is about resolving within ourselves the elements of our trauma dynamics, those we are able to work with by ourselves or with therapeutic or coaching support. Resolution means that we are less likely to be triggered, that is, our trauma dynamics activated by our relationship with our mother (and others). We can stay calm and avoid getting entangled in the tangled web.

The 'Spiral of Learning' exercises are there to help you with this reflection and resolution. You may have found them helpful so far, or decided not to do them, or at times not found them helpful. Maybe you have found other sources that help you reflect and learn about your patterns of behaving, thinking and feeling. What matters is that we all find a good way to process our experience.

Your story might be very different to some of those recounted in this section. You might have had strong emotional foundations in your life and a good relationship with your mother as an adult. You might not identify with many of the examples given. Celebrate that, while recognising that for others there is a darker element to their life story and be open to the realisation that many daughters have a very different experience which has caused them to be tightly connected in this trauma web.

While this section has looked backwards to explore the roots of our present experience, we can only change *in the present*. We can use the past to inform us, to shed light on what is happening for us in the 'here and now', on the decisions we make for ourselves and how we are entangled in the web.

We can't change the past, but can change how it continues to operate within us

Our task, if we want to go down this route, is to develop and deepen our connection with ourselves, listening to our inner voice, our body and our felt experience. This requires an emotional investment in our wellbeing, in developing our love for ourselves so that we can stop longing for it from others who can't give it to us. Then, we can begin to protect ourselves from further harmful relationships, take stock, and consider what our patterns of attachment are. Are they healthy or unhealthy? Why do we stay in unhealthy relationships? Which adapted child parts are active within us?

Blame and recrimination are not a way out of the tangled web – they are ways of staying entangled. We have to breathe into ourselves, feel our body, connect with ourselves right now. We always have choices, many of which will have consequences that may feel unwelcome, but we need to sit with these choices and not be afraid of the consequences.

Blame and recrimination are not a way out of the tangled web – they are ways of staying entangled

Like many, I have undertaken therapeutic work on my emotional trauma; it is ongoing and will be through my life. My motivation for this came primarily from my commitment to being a psychotherapist, a vehicle for many to engage in self-exploration. I then became interested in emotional trauma and how it presented in me and my clients, and in how to work with it and help others to move on from it. Your motivation will be different. It might be that you are fed up with the ongoing drama or the repeated cycles of interaction with your mother, or you recognise that you are exhausted by it, or notice how much resentment is building up in you and decide, 'Now I will change'. If you wish to make changes, where has or where will your motivation come from?

PART 4

DEVELOPING A HEALTHY RELATIONSHIP WITH YOURSELF

Personal Reflection (4)

I've noticed another survival response in me, as I have been putting this book together, in relation to how I respond to my mother and some female friends who share similar characteristics to my mother. I have become aware of the many kind and supportive actions my mother made for me as an adult. I have long dismissed these. I realised that I refused to accept these kindnesses, and I would often story them as my mother having an ulterior motive. I noticed this rejection of a possible kindly action alongside the creation of a critical narrative in relation to others too; it is a pattern. Reflecting on it, I notice that it is a narcissistic response, as the story is all about me and the impact on me.

As I have been writing this book and reflecting a lot at the same time, I am having to face up to things that I have kept hidden under an attachment to my narratives. These provided a kind of boundary, but the question for me is, "Can I let in the kind and generous actions without feeling I am letting go of my boundaries?" We all need protective boundaries, but I realise that I have often put them in a very defensive place. I obviously needed to then, but now I can review how and why I do this. Like many other daughters, I find it hard to trust the goodness of others and I don't like asking for or accepting help. I am suspicious of people's motives and that limits what goodness I can take in from others. I am now trying to open myself up.

CHAPTER 17
Reclaiming Yourself from the Influence of The Past

This section of the book is about reclaiming ourselves from elements of the lasting impact of our emotional trauma on us and on our relationship with our mother. This is an ongoing healing process. There is no end point when all is resolved, although change happens incrementally and at times suddenly. We may often find ourselves back in the thick undergrowth of our old patterns and conditioning. When that happens, we can pause, breathe deeply, settle ourselves and start again by creating new ways of being in our world.

The symbol below is that of the Celtic Spiral or 'triskel' that I referred to in Part 1, together with the idea that learning is moving up through a spiral. We come back to similar places, similar adapted and survival-self issues, and we build on the learning we experienced last time we 'met' them in our self-inquiry. Through this spiral learning we meet aspects of ourselves – our strengths and desires – that may have been repressed, lying dormant, waiting to be found. Dare we embrace them?

My understanding of the original meaning given to the Celtic Spiral is that it is about rebirth and transformation, and represents the physical, spiritual, and celestial worlds. Here I am adapting the image to symbolise the three elements of self-enquiry: 'contact with myself', 'my entangled relationship with my mother (father, other)' and 'my core essence'. These three are intertwined and we can come to our explorations through any of these into the spiral.

Reclaiming contact with myself, is about engaging with the resources in our healthy Self. These resources include creativity, imagination, curiosity, compassion, insight, the capacity to be reflective and learn from experience, the capacity to calm ourselves, to be joyful, to be able to rest and refresh ourselves. It is about listening to and trusting our inner sense of what is good for us.

Reclaiming ourselves from entanglement with our mother (or anyone else we know we are entangled with), is about moving beyond the old patterns from 'there and then' while dealing with any guilt or grief that arises as we do that. If we wish, we can relate to our mother differently, knowing that we can't change her.

'Core Essence' is the third part of reclaiming ourselves. In using the term core essence for the third spiral, I mean that which lies

202

beyond personality and our relationship with our mother. It refers to a core part of us that is vital to our sense of self, and which has been diminished by pressures or expectations within the society and family we were raised and live in. For some, it might be the feminine aspect, and reclaiming that from the restrictions or pressures that society places on women. For others it might be connected to deepening into their ancestral heritage, especially if they were born and brought up in a different culture from that of their ancestors. For example, daughters who have African or Roma heritage may wish to reclaim a connection with that, or to explore the collective traumatic history that may have been experienced. Some daughters may consider their core essence to be about deepening their 'soul connection' or related to a spiritual exploration.

You may know already what your core essence is about, or it may be an aspect of your being that, for whatever reasons, you have not explored. If you are not sure what it is, a helpful developmental question is: *"What is the third element of the learning spiral that connects deeply for me and will be a guide to my life?"* Whatever focus we give it, it is a valuable addition to our development, and is about reclaiming ourselves at a more soulful or mysterious level, one that can enable transformation on many levels.

The road to reclaiming ourselves is often bumpy, messy, distressing and frustrating. At times we might want to give up on it. The choice is always ours. For me, though, there is no other road to travel. We can be helped along the way by finding guides — whether they are therapists, good friends or books and online courses — by being in the company of, or in a community with people on a similar road, and through our personal qualities of curiosity, self-compassion, patience, self-respect and self-honouring. As I write about this journey, I feel it is important to reiterate that it is an ongoing process for me, and for most people who choose this path. Each step forward I make, I feel a loosening of the binds and a reclaiming of myself, which is motivation enough for me to continue. My process includes keeping a reflective journal, participating in relevant online webinars and programmes, talking with others who understand, and teaching (always a good stimulus to keep on track). I know what some of the 'theoretical' answers are, but I am regularly unable to apply them to myself some of the time. If this is ever your experience, I join you in that and we are not alone. Whilst teachers of all kinds can help us, we need to find our own answers. It is a journey, and like all journeys, sometimes it is uncomfortable and at other times, the view is wonderful. In the next few chapters, I offer some thoughts about what this process involves together with reflections on some of the challenges.

CHAPTER 18
Honouring and Resourcing Yourself

One of the dangers of these final chapters is that it could feel
to the reader as if all the self-awareness work suggested is very
straightforward, as long as we work at it hard enough. What an unhealthy message that would be! On the other hand, unless we set
out to do what we can, when we can, to learn about and change
aspects of our beliefs, thoughts, and behaviour we will remain
locked in our tangled web. It is important not to berate ourselves
if we take time to put changes in place. The process should feel
kindly and compassionate.

Honouring and resourcing ourselves are key to any reclaiming process and to untangling or stepping out of the web. Some
daughters were honoured and resourced as children, so have
taken those abilities into their lives as adults. Other daughters
with negative, controlling, narcissistic, absent or emotionally unavailable mothers, may not have experienced much honouring and
resourcing as children or did so only occasionally and/or spas-
modically. Maybe we felt honoured and respected by others, who
also offered us opportunities to resource ourselves. Enhancing

how we honour and resource ourselves is a key step in being able to change our inner processes and outer relationships.

If we honour someone, we treat them with respect, admiration and fulfil any obligations to them – I am suggesting we do just that to ourselves. Honouring our intuition, our felt experience, our inner knowledge of what is healthy for us, and our self-understanding is the way we can steer our reclaiming process. Alongside honouring, we need to resource ourselves through activities that help us feel fully alive, that feed this healthy part of ourselves and give it strength to grow. Honouring needs resourcing, and resourcing needs honouring. They reinforce each other.

One of the challenges of pulling back from our old patterns of relating is that we can think this is being selfish. Many of us were programmed to believe that we had to sacrifice our needs and energy for the benefit of others; we don't. In putting our own healthy needs first, we won't get entangled, and we can also be kind, caring and compassionate to others if we wish.

Another challenge we may need to face is a deep unconscious fear from childhood fantasy, that if we become more of ourselves and no longer entangled, we may kill off our mother or even die ourselves. This isn't the case. Honouring ourselves involves separating from our mother, so we become two distinct people rather than the entangled women we were, and in so doing we see each other more fully. Far from dying ourselves, we experience more energy and we become more enlivened. Unless we can truly believe this, it is hard to make the shift from dishonouring to honouring ourselves.

Honouring needs resourcing, and resourcing needs honouring. They reinforce each other

As women, we have probably also been 'claimed' by societal expectations and judgements, as our mothers were before us. Women are told in the media and often in workplaces, how they should or shouldn't look; what they should and shouldn't do or say; how they should and shouldn't behave. The message often given is that it is not okay to be ourselves. We learn that it is shameful to talk about any mental health or disability problems we have had or continue to have. We can be shamed about our body and how we look. As a result, we keep things hidden if we can, which takes energy away from living fully. Reclaiming ourselves from any shame we have been made to carry and from these judgements of others is often difficult – we have buried it so deep and done so much to adapt and fit in. We don't need to add to this dishonouring by blaming ourselves for this, and we can honour ourselves by feeling compassion for what we had to do to survive.

Reclaiming ourselves involves honouring our own strengths, talents, resources and energies and differentiating those from how we were conditioned or trained to think about them. This often involves reconnecting with any of our strengths and talents that had to be suppressed or silenced as they weren't welcomed or encouraged by those around us. It is also about how we talk about and to ourselves, and the self-beliefs we hold. Reorientating ourselves in this way can be challenging. It takes curiosity and courage.

Spiral of Learning

Stop for a moment and reflect on what 'honouring yourself' means for you. Make some notes on this in your journal.

Reflect on the times you have honoured yourself and what it felt like. Write down the key words that come to you as you do this.

Many of us are so used to not honouring ourselves, or of only doing so randomly, that we may not realise what it means for us in everyday terms. To illustrate the difference between honouring and dishonouring I have developed two lists of types of behaviour and thoughts, expressed as personal statements. These are suggestions to help us raise awareness of where on the spectrum of honouring to dishonouring we may be. Some of us may be nearer one end than the other. I place myself somewhere in the middle, with trips down the dishonouring end when I lose contact with myself. I wish I could say this wasn't very often, but that would not be the truth.

Honouring ourselves:
- *I feel secure and confident in myself*
- *I believe in myself and my worth as a person in this family and world*
- *I claim all my talents and I let go of those I have carried forward for others (particularly parents)*
- *I value, am curious about and explore the talents or interests that I have but which weren't developed, as others didn't value them*

- *I treat my body well, allowing it to rest; I eat well and get the movement I need*
- *I can 'hold' myself emotionally. If I am upset or anxious, I can calm myself and be with my feelings without getting overwhelmed or rushing to action to escape them*
- *I have the right to say no, and do say no when what I am being asked involves a self-sacrifice I do not want to make*
- *I take account of my healthy needs in my decision making*

Dishonouring ourselves:

- *I believe I am not good enough as I am*
- *I worry about what others think of me and try to adjust to them, even if that means limiting myself*
- *I keep myself small, so I won't upset anyone and/or my mother won't be envious of me, or so that I don't show up my sister/ brother*
- *I am self-critical, I have regular negative thoughts about myself; I can also be judgmental of others*
- *I diminish myself in all kinds of ways*
- *I feel I 'have to' do things when I don't want to*
- *I put my needs way down the list in relation to those of others*
- *I use my energy in ways that exhaust me rather than enliven me*
- *I don't attend to my health and wellbeing*

Spiral of Learning

Where are you on the Spectrum of Honouring Yourself?

Not at all   *All the time*

_____

What do you notice when you reflect on that?

If you recognise that honouring yourself is not a strength within you yet, you can decide to make the shift from non-honouring to honouring. It is hard to get out of tangled webs of relationships until we have developed this capacity.

Steps Towards Honouring Ourselves

- **Our first step** is to become aware of the habits we have established, the thoughts and behaviour responses that keep 'dishonouring' in place.
- **The second step** is to use our understanding of emotional trauma to see how our adapted child parts are active and what they are trying to defend us from; that is, what our inner fears from childhood are.
- **The third step** is to put different thoughts and behaviours in place. We can achieve this through personal reflection and a genuine commitment to ourselves and to what is healthy for us.
- **The fourth step** is to be self-compassionate and caring of ourselves if and when we return to dishonouring; to comfort ourselves and start again with step one. Remember this is a spiral of learning.

Our 'Felt' Experience

A challenge for some of us in self-reflection and self-awareness is our capacity to connect with our body and what is called our 'felt experience' – that is, when we connect with parts of our body that may feel numb or vibrant, strong or weak or tingling, aching, or anxious; when we can locate where in our body we experience a particular emotion, such as sadness or anger. Being able to connect with this 'felt experience' gives us additional information that we can process in our adult brains, which we can reflect on and make associations with that bring us insight. This inner experience comes from our intrinsic memory, bypassing our thoughts which often come from our old patterns of surviving. When we have information from this felt experience, we can then process that with our minds. Without it, we don't have all the data we need to honour ourselves.

Emotional trauma can affect our capacity to access this information. If we are aware that we find it hard to feel into our body, we can learn how to how to do it. Sarah noticed this: *"I find it really hard to be in connection with my body; I can't do those embodiment exercises where you are asked to share what you are experiencing in your body. I understand why. I am doing short exercises so that I can build up my ability to do this."* When I started psychotherapy training, I found it hard to connect with my 'felt experience' too; I didn't understand what people were talking about. I thought they were making it up. Over the years, having participated in body-based therapies, I now have no problem with it at all. I also noticed that to begin with, I didn't really trust what I was experiencing. This can be a challenge for many of us, particularly where our feelings were not validated or were ignored as children, but we can build up trust in what we feel when we recognise this is part of reclaiming ourselves and our experience.

Having been physically or sexually abused can add deep complications to our relationship with our body. Instead of being nurtured, our body was hurt, bruised, damaged and taken from us in the abuse. Such daughters may feel their body let them down by not resisting or running away. This is false thinking. The trauma response that kicked in to protect them may have produced numbness, a frozen state and shut down any messages from the body. This is natural and may well have saved them at the time. It was not their body that let them down but the abuser who harmed them. For these daughters, sensitive therapy can help them reclaim their body and not be overwhelmed by their felt experiences.

We can build up trust in what we feel when we recognise this is part of reclaiming ourselves

Resourcing ourselves means doing enough of the things that leave us feeling alive and bring joy or calmness. This involves having the support of loving people around us, who want the best for us – and to remove ourselves from those who don't. We need the company of good friends, those we really connect with, who will listen to us and who may help us change our perspective – as we will with them. We also need to resource ourselves through getting enough rest, stimulation and joyful activity. Some daughters will find this easy and will come to it naturally. The rest of us are unlikely to have prioritised these activities in our lives, as we were too busy rescuing, protecting, over-working or in other ways caught up with our emotional trauma.

Resourcing also involves activities that stimulate our imagination, refresh us, calm us and bring us joy such as walking in the countryside or parks, sitting by a river, dancing, being where lots of people are doing interesting things, listening to or playing music, or picking up some coloured pens and creating an image. Some find meditation, mindfulness and deep breathing exercises beneficial to calm an anxious mind and to bring us into a better connection with ourselves. Yoga or tai-chi involve a connection with the body and similarly can be resourcing. The possibilities are endless.

Resourcing ourselves means doing enough of the things that make us feel alive and which bring joy or calmness

Small Steps to Resourcing Ourselves

- **Slow down:** The first step is to slow down, especially if we are programmed to rush around taking responsibility for doing things that are not ours to resolve. We all need periods of quiet reflection or rest from which our core energy can emerge and we have to create space to dedicate to this process.
- **Feel it**: The second step on the path of resourcing ourselves is to know it when we feel it. Connecting with those feelings of joy, energy or truly resting. This helps us identify what we can put on our list of 'things that resource me'
- **Experiment**: The third step is to experiment with what gives us joy and fun and a sense of vitality, and to do more of it. Some of us may need to learn how to rest and to rest in our bodies, this may include finding the best place to do this. While doing this, watching out for the inner voice that chastises us

and tells us to 'do *something useful*" or that we will *"never be successful."*

- **Observation**: The fourth step is to notice when we have let go of resourcing ourselves and returned to old patterns of behaviour. If this is the case, we can practise self-compassion and then start again. It is all part of the same spiral.

I admit that resourcing myself is a challenge a lot of the time. I know I share this trait with others who are also too busy rushing around, pushing our bodies almost to breaking point, dishonouring ourselves and consequently unable to rest or relax. If you find resting in your body easy, you may wonder what I am talking about as this is already an intrinsic part of your life; if so, celebrate that. Others of us can take up the challenge of observing how we don't or can't do that, and then experiment with ways that slow us down and create situations that give us joy.

Spiral of Learning

You may already know exactly the things that resource you. Are you doing enough of them? If not, what needs to happen for you to have more of this in your life?

Maybe you have never been given the opportunities as a child or taken them as an adult to find out what resources you, at a deep level within. Perhaps you have told yourself that there is nothing available to you or in your self-talk you might hear the voices of your mother, father, your teachers or others. Try to silence them and just list as many things as you can that you think may be resourcing for you.

There are no rules here, you can put whatever you like on the list. Then you can go back through the list and highlight 3 that you might experiment with. If you find this challenging, stay calm and curious, this is all part of the reclaiming process.

If you have become numb to the sensations of aliveness and vitality, of joy and rest try to notice when you do feel a sense of feeling resourced, no matter how small. What are you doing? Who is with you? Where are you? Is there an activity involved, and if so, what? Catch these sensations, however fleeting, and build on them.

Here are some short exercises that you may find helpful if you want to feel more connection with your body. You can set yourself ten minutes a day to practise.
  - *It starts with the breath. Focus on your breathing, and slow*

down the out breath. Breathe in for the count of 5 and out for 7, 8, 9, or 10.

- *Now feel your feet firmly on the ground and your bottom on the chair (assuming you are sitting, otherwise just feel your feet on the ground and your legs keeping you standing).*
- *Focus on a part of your body you are aware of, maybe your hands or your shoulders, any part of your body that you have a felt connection with. Just 'breathe' into that area, this is a way of imaging your breath is going to those places.*
- *If you have no sense of connection with a part of your body, just keep with the breathing and see what emerges. Give it time.*
- *If you do have a felt connection with some of your body, move your focus for example from your hands to your wrists and arms, or from your shoulders to your neck or arms.*

You can also do a simple body scan, after you have settled into your breathing you can imagine yourself starting at your toes, and working up through your feet, ankles, lower legs, knees, thighs and so on up to the top of your head. You can notice which bits feel numb, which bits feel alive, which bits you have no real feeling sensation from.

When writing up your Reflective Journal, you could pause, put your pen down, do the breathing and see what emotion arises in you from what you have been writing. Maybe you feel agitation, or calmness or fear. Then identify where in your body you feel that. Maybe your sternum, your belly, your legs. Focus on that feeling and that body area. Just sit with it and see what arises.

CHAPTER 19
Engaging Your Inner Resources of Creativity and Curiosity

Our capacity for engaging our creativity and curiosity, without judgement, is part of reclaiming ourselves. These are resources within our healthy Self and available to us all. We might express our creativity very differently but using our imagination and having new ideas and implementing them is part of living life with vitality. We need curiosity for our self-development and therefore learning and change.

Being Curious

Think of children of two or three years old, always asking 'why?' and wanting to explore everything. A baby's curiosity starts very early; as she brings her eyes into focus on those around her, as she plays with her feet and hands exploring her body, and as she plays with toys. Curiosity is our doorway to learning and development. As children though, our natural curiosity may not have been welcomed or encouraged. Some of us might have been told 'curiosity killed the cat', or perhaps those around us didn't have the time or emotional space to indulge our explorations. Maybe their curiosity had been diminished by their parents. We might have been too traumatised ourselves to be able to be curious, or we feared what punishments might follow. Perhaps at school there were teachers who ridiculed our curiosity and creativity, leaving us feeling humiliated and shamed. Some of us might have learnt therefore to 'switch off' our curiosity resource and become afraid of accessing and engaging with it. It remains with us though, and we can switch in on again.

We need to engage our curiosity if we are to become fully ourselves and explore our felt experience and if we are to know more about what has shaped our behaviour, beliefs and emotions. Curiosity is essential for personal change. Our Reflective Journals are an exercise in curiosity.

Curiosity is our doorway to learning and development

Our Creativity and Imagination

Play is so important to a child's development, and many of us were fortunate to be able to play a lot, and were encouraged and supported to create pictures, to model with clay, write stories or act in plays. Maybe we had some great companions from an early age with whom we developed our ability to play. Look in any school for the under elevens in the UK and you will see how play and creativity is showcased. At one stage in my career, I was training to teach English, Drama and Art to 8-13 year-old children. I had to do a project with them for my assessment. It turned out to be a highlight in my creative life as we as a class, made masks and wrote stories, and put on a little play which involved everyone in the group. There was some amazingly creative activity. Some children found it hard to step into the imaginal space, but they all found a way to be involved. I am deeply grateful to all of them for showing me what I was capable of, too. Regrettably, my creative spirit closed over again for some years as I moved away from working with children.

Play can be messy, using materials that need cleaning up and some daughters were never allowed to make a mess. Others weren't given a quiet space to be creative, as they were required to help with the childcare of siblings or were told to 'do something sensible'. Some may have been given too much space through being left alone without much to play with. Perhaps play was limited by rules and restrictions, or the outcome of play or creativity was criticised or met with disappointment or disapproval. Perhaps the family system 'didn't do play' or was under so much stress that playing was hard. If so, daughters may have forgotten how to be playful and believe they have no creativity or imagination or lack confidence in their ideas and creative energy. However, creativity brings hope and change. If we are afraid of change, because we are afraid of failure or abandonment, then we stifle our own creativity and therefore, our life energy.

To express our creativity as children is to become fully ourselves; as we experiment and learn from the creative process, we discover what we love to do and what talents we have. Where this is not encouraged, we may give up on ourselves and just follow the rules or the restrictions that are placed on us. We might have learnt to say no to the natural direction of our life energy and thus our ability to create. The good news is that our life energy doesn't go away nor does our ability to create a life of vitality for ourselves. We can always commit to helping ourselves reconnect with it.

If we are afraid of change, because we are afraid of failure or abandonment, then we stifle our own creativity and therefore, our life energy

It is easy to see how our confidence and enjoyment in our creativity can be diminished or dimmed by our early experiences and relationships. For some daughters, however, there can be even greater impacts on their creativity and imagination through emotional trauma from negative, narcissistic or cruel mothers, and particularly those who were unable to contain their maternal ambivalence. This not only diminishes our engagement with both creativity and curiosity but can also result in a particular trauma survival dynamic within us.

Previously, I talked of 'adaptive survival parts', that is bundles of thoughts, beliefs, emotions, and actions, that operate within us. One of these that may be present within some daughters is a dynamic which results in our being persecutory towards our own creativity and curiosity. It might seem odd that we should do this to ourselves, but it carries the negative or destructive energy from our mother, other key caregivers or our school teachers, who were unable to support our natural creativity and curiosity as children; who instead told us our paintings were terrible, or to stop asking questions. It is possible that they were unable to access their own creativity and had no idea of how to help us nurture ours. We learnt that this was how to treat our curiosity and creativity; we learnt not to trust or honour it. We judge ourselves before anyone else has the chance to. It means we can be cruel to ourselves.

'My experience of this dynamic within me is that it kills off my creativity, depressing my self-belief and exhausting me. Then another voice within me activates, and I berate myself for my lack of creativity and energy. I notice this energy comes out when I am tired and feeling vulnerable. I seem to allow my energetic spirit to die by doubting myself and my voice. I realise that unless I focus on restorative energy, I can't stand up to this inner part of me.'
– Personal reflection

As children, we can take in this negative energy from any adult but is is most likely to be our closest care giver, who in most cases is our mother. It may come from overt behaviour or from more subtle forms of undermining our self-confidence or imagination. For some it may come from the mother's inability to manage her ambivalence and her impulse to be cruel and abusive. We may recognise that our mother – and perhaps her mother before her – seemed to carry this destructive energy. Sometimes the links are clear but when they are not, we don't need to keep looking for explanations; we know from our inner experience if we have that internal dynamic or not and whether it forms one of the knots in our web.

Why might our creativity and curiosity be attacked? It could be that the mother or caretaker who either attacks it directly or is unable to foster and encourage it, fears her daughter's creativity and her emergence as 'her own person'. Perhaps the mother's mother did the same, so as Russian Dolls it is carried down through our ancestors. It could be that our creative energy reminds our mother of her unfulfilled life, and it is too emotionally painful for her to tolerate it. Some mothers' stories are that they had wanted to have a creative, artistic career but were forbidden from pursuing that by a parent. Their pain at this loss may lead them to be unable to offer artistic play to their daughters and may dismiss any poetry, paintings or clay modelling that their daughters may bring home from school.

Another reason may be linked with the idea that creative people often challenge the status quo in society, and thereby the family system, and so creativity may be feared or silenced. If children get 'too curious' in a family system with secrets or which is unable to foster curiosity, they will learn quickly that it is not a welcome trait. Our creative energy is also diminished by living in traumatising or highly stressed environments. The hormones we produce in response to such a context have an impact on how we learn and create, making it harder for us to concentrate and focus. Our imagination is dimmed.

Sometimes the links are clear but when they are not, we don't need to keep looking for explanations; we know from our inner experience if we have that internal dynamic or not and whether it forms one of the knots in our web

This capacity to kill off our own creativity and curiosity is the opposite of being our own loving mother, as it is destructive, sucking out life-energy and bringing self-doubt and self-hatred. Marion Woodman, a Jungian Psychoanalyst called this dynamic an expression of the 'death mother' archetype, as it can have such a destructive effect on our life spirit. When this inner dynamic is present it can seem that there is no hope, and our ability to feel and be creative disappears. This may happen when we are starting something new that we want to do, and the dark energy does its best to kill it off. We attack ourselves through negative thoughts that bring despair with them, and then blame ourselves for being as we are. My experience of it is: *'This dynamic comes to the foreground when I am working and struggling with a new project or facing the types of obstacles that life often throws up. And yet, I know from experience that I am a good problem solver, that I do find my way through, and when I remember that, I can regain a hold on hope. When caught in the dark dynamic though, that memory is erased temporarily.'*

When in the grip of this, we may treat ourselves in a cold way with no compassion and may say things like, *"Why did I ever think I would be able to do that?"* or, *"I am too lazy to achieve anything"*; *"I am wasting my time; I will never amount to anything"; 'I am deluded about my talents".* While the internal critic is a common experience of many daughters, often taken in from external critics, it doesn't always carry the same level of destruction to our imagination. Those affected can come to feel imprisoned by their own sense of inadequacy.

Not all daughters have internalised this way of attacking their creative energy. Those of us who have are likely to find the criticism comes in waves – it isn't there all the time but can suddenly appear when we are engaging in a new project. Some of the indicators that this dynamic is operating within in us, include:

- We may give up our hopes and dreams, our aspirations and creative endeavours, through persuading ourselves there is no point, or that we can't do it, or it costs too much (include here any other statements that dismisses our intentions)

- We may use cruel self-talk and express self-hatred
- We might have a sense of giving up on **our** life and **our** uniqueness
- We might feel ambivalent about a lot of things, unable to make a full connection with what **we** want for ourselves
- Alongside this we may feel waves of despair and loss of hope, with everything feeling worthless or a waste of time, a bit like depression

All this can create a sense of paralysis or of being imprisoned, unable to move forward or to think clearly. The impact on our life spirit can also show itself through ambivalence, as if we have given up trying to imagine and determine our own life. We may feel inadequate when we are invited to follow our passion, perhaps thinking – *"I don't feel passionate about anything"* and having other negative thoughts about ourselves. For some of us, passion might not be the right word, but the essence is the answer to the questions – *"What makes me feel fully myself? What do I need in my life? What do I love being part of?"* – these questions aren't about careers or jobs, but about what it is that brings us joy, inspiration and connection. The fundamental question we need to ask ourselves, when we come to an authentic answer about our passions is, *"Can I stay with that without telling myself it's impossible, or that I'd fail?"*

If our mother is still alive and continues to fuel these dynamics, then they are repeatedly given new life. We can protect ourselves from this by committing to loving ourselves enough to put boundaries in place, so we can refuse to take in negative messages from our mother. Protecting ourselves also comes from developing our self-awareness of when we are in the grip of these destructive dynamics within, and developing strategies for moving away from it. We also can learn that it does pass, as long as we are able to resource ourselves.

We can protect ourselves from the destructive dynamics within by developing strategies for moving away from it.

As young children, we are likely to have had the natural vibrancy that all children have. If this was crushed along with our creativity, we may have taken this in as a 'given' at a time when we couldn't fight back, and we couldn't protect ourselves. Now we are adults, we can recognise this dynamic for what it is and reduce its power over us; we can love ourselves, want and protect ourselves; we don't need to stay imprisoned in these dynamics.

Engaging our creativity

We may need to foster and resource our creativity and imagination as a loving mother would with her young child, so that we can strengthen it. Many of us may need to learn how to play and explore what activities bring a sense of playing where **our** energies want to take us. We can turn to creative pursuits purely because it brings us joy and provides an outlet for our imagination. Maybe we learnt about playing again through our children or grandchildren or our work.

I love studio space. I am not a talented artist by most assessments, and I would never win any awards, but I love playing with paint, preferably in a studio with others. There is something about the freedom of the space and being with others who are being creative. Some may produce things of great beauty, but we all can enjoy the process – and produce things that have meaning and importance to us. There are all kinds of other ways we can help foster our creativity. I love dancing wildly at music gigs and one thing I regret about getting older is that these opportunities are fewer and further between. I find dancing restores energy and spontaneity.

The point here is that we are not being creative to win approval or to become the favoured child, we are enjoying a free-flowing process that comes from within us. This might be dance, or image making, or music, or writing, or sewing, or gardening, or a work project – the possibilities are extensive. Think of a small child jumping up and down in a puddle of water, loving the impact she is having on the water; or a child planting seeds and feeling her connection with what grows. Play is an essential part of life. The important thing is that it has no duty or work associations, even though we may be paid for the outcomes.

I have often reflected on why I love studio space and concluded that partly it is because it is 'outside' the rules of other space. We can make a mess, get paint or chalk or clay on our hands and apron; there is often silence interspersed with moments of conversation; there are no demands on us to attend to others. The 'studio space' maybe a helpful image to hold, because we need to create a space like this within our own psyches, free from the constraints that have been imposed on us by others, including our mothers. Our ideal creative space will be unique to each of us, as is what gives us joy and hope.

We are not being creative to get approval or to become the favoured child, we are enjoying a free-flowing process that comes from within us

If we are aware we have the destructive dynamic operating within us at times, creating ways to restore our wellbeing and belief in ourselves is how to step out of those self-limiting responses to our creativity. If we feel any of the indicators emerging as we begin a creative process, we can remind ourselves that they belong to the past, they are not about the present and not about us, nor about our creativity.

Living creatively is a way of life, it is about a mindset and attitude that is free from the restrictions and possible attacks from our childhood, which may have continued into adulthood. Some daughters find their creative spirit in their paid work, as I did with teaching. I have worked with some incredibly creative people in all lines of work, people who allow their creative flair to turn something from the mundane into being alive and vibrant. It isn't all about art or dancing or writing, it is how we live our life. It is about how we approach our tasks and what energy, colour and creativity we bring to them. We can regain our childlike enthusiasm for life, for **our** life.

Spiral of Learning

Spiral of Change
- *What are you most curious about right now? It can be about anything. List out 2 or 3 things you are really curious about.*
- *Pick one and create a 'To Do' list with ideas on how you can fulfil your curiosity about this issue/area.*

Reflect on times in your past when you have felt your creative energy flowing. Bring to mind a time when this happened, like I did whilst working with those children in my teaching practice.
- *What were you doing?*
- *Who else was there?*
- *Was it a quiet space or were you creative within a group?*
- *How did you feel while you were doing it?*
- *What made it so special?*
- *What internal resources were you drawing on?*

Imagine you are living with your creativity fully active.
- *What are you doing?*
- *Who with?*
- *Write it down is if you were writing a story about a woman like you e.g. 'Hannah is fully in touch with her creative spirit. She..."*

How could you have more of this in your life? Write down three or four things you could do, create or bring into your life, right now which would bring your creative spirit even more alive. Maybe you have had some ideas in the past which have been shelved as 'not possible'? How about re-engaging with them and letting your imagination flow to see what happens?

You may need to create more space in your life to enable you to engage in these ways. This is also part of the creative spirit; finding and bringing about ways in which you can play, dream and let your imagination flow without interruption. What is your version of studio space?

Notice as you do these exercises if you are aware of a negative voice emerging, telling you not to be ridiculous, or diminishing or undermining your ideas and hopes. If you do, imagine yourself saying to that inner voice, 'Please go into another room for now. I am busy and enjoying doing this.' You may need to practise this and feel free to make up a sentence that works for you.

CHAPTER 20
Saying 'No' to Others and 'Yes' to Ourselves

Saying 'No' to others and 'Yes' to our inner self is part of honouring and reclaiming. Saying no is about honouring our boundaries and protecting ourselves from entanglement and the suffering that can go with it. Too often, many of us say yes to others when we would rather say no, but for various reasons, feel we can't. This can be accompanied by not saying yes to our own experience, truth, talents and resources, and our needs for healthy emotional living, thereby continuing the conditioning and training we had as a child.

Saying no to others at one level can come through 'healthy anger'. If someone behaves inappropriately our anger helps us push back, defending ourselves; this is part of the fight or flight response. It protects us. Anger doesn't have to be acted on with an angry response, although if I was being attacked in the street, I would want to be full of anger and rage and express that fully.

For the reasons raised in previous chapters, many of us have grown up afraid of anger and confrontation. However, anger that comes up in our relationships, including our mother, is valuable information indicating that we are being invited to accept something that feels dishonouring. It is data and as such we can notice and acknowledge it. If we remain afraid or ashamed of it, we cut off our access to that information. Often, I have heard women describe a situation and say, *"I found it so frustrating"* and if I push against that they may then say, *"Yes I was angry, but I don't want to be angry about it."* This blocks the anger before it can be felt, processed and used as information. There is nothing wrong with acknowledging that we feel angry in our relationships; the problem comes if we have no impulse control or act out of that anger in harmful ways.

Saying 'No' to others and 'Yes' to our inner self is part of honouring and reclaiming

Feeling that edge of anger can help us learn not to say yes when we mean no – as can checking-in with our felt experience, to give us a chance to notice if we do really want to say yes, or not. Often our programming kicks in immediately and we find our old patterns reactivated, finding that we have said yes to something before we have even considered it. Those of us who rescue, protect, are compulsive helpers or family heroes regularly find ourselves saying yes when we really mean no. We may respond so quickly, due to habits of a life-time and because we carry the dishonouring belief that we have no choice. The challenge is to break this circuit.

Those of us who rescue, protect, are compulsive helpers or family heroes regularly find ourselves saying yes when we really mean no

Saying YES when we mean NO, results in feelings of resentment or being put upon and our energy is instantly deflated. It also re-fuels our inner anger. Up until now, we may never have practised saying NO instead of YES. It may be new territory for us and one that we can step into enthusiastically.

Spiral of Learning

Dr Gabor Maté, a Hungarian-Canadian physician, shared the following exercise which I have found useful, and I hope you will too. He advises we do it regularly each week, or even each day if it is a strong habit we have...

Ask yourself:

- *Where in this last week, did I not say 'No' when I had a 'No' ready to say?*
- *What was the impact on me, emotionally and physically?*
- *What were my beliefs that stopped me saying 'No'? These may reflect:*

    A compulsive concern with the needs of others over our own

    A compulsive identification with duty and responsibility

    A belief that I can never disappoint any one or that I am responsible for how others feel

    A belief that otherwise I won't be seen or the hope that it may bring some love

You may recognise the underlying beliefs in this exercise as coming from your adapted child; her longing for love, closeness and recognition coupled with her fear of retribution if she claims her own boundaries. Dr Maté suggests we do this exercise weekly or more frequently. It can help bring us more into contact with ourselves and can break our habitual ways of being entangled with others.

The last part of this exercise is:
- *"What am I not saying 'Yes' to, when there is a 'Yes' to be said, in relation to honouring and reclaiming myself?"*

So long as we keep on saying yes to others when we mean no, our energies are dissipated and we are locked into dishonouring patterns. Saying YES to ourselves includes engaging in the activities that resource us, and reclaiming those strengths, talents and quirkinesses that aren't always welcomed or encouraged by those around us. It also includes speaking our own truth rather than colluding with the narrative of others.

We now know that adapting to our caregivers as children often required us to suppress or smother strengths and talents that weren't welcomed or encouraged. Such strengths might include our intelligence, creativity, curiosity, our uniqueness in how we saw the world, our quietness or noisiness, or things we were interested in. Sometimes money might have been in short supply, meaning the opportunity to develop skills when we were young wasn't possible. Whatever the reason, we learnt to suppress our talents.

Saying YES to ourselves is part of honouring and reclaiming ourselves

As adults, we may have an intuitive sense of what these talents and strengths might be, or we can use our curiosity and courage to explore what might be there waiting to be found. We can open up the 'box' that they have been packed away in, and be inquisitive about what is in there, deciding what we want to reclaim and how to integrate this into our lives, now.

Conversely, many of us were told what talents and strengths we were expected to develop to serve the vision our parents had for us. We had little option other than to be compliant as children. Reclaiming ourselves is about letting go of anything that doesn't fit well with our true sense of ourselves. Maybe we were 'trained' to be a certain way in the world and have just followed that programming until one day we think, *"This isn't my life, this isn't what I want to do."* We might even, by that stage, have become successful in using that training or we may have struggled for years trying to be something we are not. I have had many conversations with women in a coaching context, in which some struggled to continue deploying the talents they had been told they had but didn't really have a liking for. Some wanted to explore other avenues but felt they should or ought to continue in what they had been 'trained' to fulfil. Some women went into professional work arenas to please a parent rather than themselves. Sometimes the 'rebel' child will do what she knows will annoy her mother or father the most, and this may not necessarily be what her own energy directs her towards.

A British paediatrician, Donald Winnicott (1896–1971), talked of 'the true and false self'; the true self being our talents, resources, aptitudes and character that makes us fully ourselves. The false self is the mask we wear and adaptations we had to make to fit in and not to be abandoned. Emotional trauma causes such a split between our true and false selves, which I have referred to in this book as the healthy Self and adapted parts. Saying yes to ourselves is about scrutinising these survival thoughts, self-beliefs, resources and talents and assessing whether they are expressions of being healthy in ourselves or are about meeting the needs and requirements of others.

If we say yes to ourselves, we can take up our rightful place in the world. That is, we don't need to make ourselves 'invisible' out of fear of what might follow if we don't. Some daughters might have deliberately kept themselves small and denied their talents or intelligence so as not to provoke their mother's envy, disappointment or hostility. The challenge for a daughter who did this is to set about reclaiming all she gave up to protect her mother. In addition to this silencing of ourselves, most women, including our mothers have learnt that society expects us to 'know our place' which is often to keep quiet and diminish our talents.

We are saying no to ourselves if we have spent a lifetime trying to prove our right to exist, for example, working hard, sacrificing ourselves, pleasing people, or fitting in. Beneath these are talents and strengths which have been turned to the service of our survival defences, out of fear of abandonment. Reclaiming ourselves is about disentangling from them and using them in the service of self-honouring instead. We often call on our willpower to push ourselves, to press on regardless. We mistake it for our free will. Willpower, pushing ourselves, is at times beneficial, however when it becomes a habitual way of living it exhausts and diminishes us. Our will comes from our healthy Self; it is what we want for ourselves to support our curiosity, vitality, joy, rest, creativity and courage. Honouring ourselves is to metaphorically stand to our full height, straight backed, firm on the ground, knowing we have a right to the space we have claimed.

We may want to reclaim our body from the judgements of others, to let go of the 'truths' we have held on to for a long time, for example, about having 'fat legs' or a 'big bottom'. We may want to step beyond any shame we have carried for being different or humiliated by others. We can do this by telling ourselves, repeatedly, that we have a right to exist just as we are. We may want to say a big YES to our sexuality however we experience that. Our personal development task is to untangle what is ours but has been suppressed, and what we have been required to take on and we want to let go of.

Spiral of Learning

It can be very useful in honouring and resourcing yourself, to determine your talents and that which you are saying yes and no to out of past programming. Answering these questions may be helpful in that respect:

- *What talents do I have that I do not honour?*
- *What talents or strengths are waiting for me to liberate and welcome?*
- *To what extent am I carrying the expectations of my mother (or father) in how I live my life?*
- *In what ways, if at all, am I driven to fulfil expectations that have little to do with me?*
- *What talents do I have that do not bring me joy and while they pleased my mother/father I would like now to stop or change so they fit my inner sense of myself much better?*

In the previous chapter I listed statements that are connected with honouring and dishonouring ourselves. I noticed that I had made the dishonouring list somewhat longer – clearly it was more familiar to me. In that dishonouring list were many negative self-beliefs by which we say no to ourselves. The ones in the honouring list are beliefs that instead say "Yes! This is me."

- *Make a list of the positive knowledge you have about yourself, that feels true and honouring and to which you are prepared to say YES to.*

Facing our Truth

While reclaiming and honouring are actions full of challenges, which we can choose to rise to if we wish, many find 'facing our truth' one of the toughest challenges of all. This is because we have learnt to deny it for so long, and to replace it with illusion; to constantly distract ourselves from it, to distort it, or from a sense of shame, are unable to speak it; or it has never felt safe enough to tell the truth of who we really are, deep down, beneath all the lived experiences of our lives.

A definition of resilience I like is that it is having the resources to face reality without collapse. When we feel emotionally overwhelmed we can collapse into ourselves, feeling helpless and powerless. Building up our healthy resources allows us to face our truth, the reality of our experience and to stay with it without being overwhelmed by it. It means we are no longer afraid of it, nor hiding from it. It may be something we have to slowly work towards, or that we need to find a safe space with someone we trust to speak of it. If we are not sufficiently resourced it can be a deeply painful experience.

Facing our truth is about not being a 'walking victim'. It is about owning our experiences and being able to say, from our mature Self, *"My mother hit me and hurt me. I was very frightened, and I carry that wound within me."* Or *"My father was a violent man. I saw him hit my mother and my sister. I carry that within me."* Or, *"As a child I didn't feel wanted or seen. I carry that within me"*; or *"My mother left me; she wasn't able to be a mother to me, and I carry that within me."* Saying this acknowledges those hurt, wounded and betrayed parts within our emotional trauma. I have reflected in previous chapters how in denial I was, and what a shock it was to me to realise that the reality of my childhood was different to how I was choosing the perceive it. When the shock diminished, I realised it was freeing to face my truth. As Alice Miller tells us, with the title of her book, *The Truth Will Set Us Free,* the truth frees us from all the contortions we have performed, psychologically and behaviourally, to pretend the reality was different.

Facing our truth is about not being a 'walking victim'

One of the challenges is that we may find it hard to believe our truth. Our habit of denial is so great that we doubt ourselves, doubt our experiences and doubt our right to express them. This is where accessing our intrinsic memory through our felt experience becomes so important. When the truth is spoken, we feel it in our body, we have a resonance with it. If it remains just an idea or a story, it doesn't have that same connection. Some years ago, there was much disquiet about so called 'false memory syndrome'. The accusation was that some therapists were planting ideas in clients' imagination, which the individual then claimed as a memory, or that individuals were creating a fantasy about what happened to them. This mostly related to sexual abuse. It is possible that such things do happen. It is also possible that in some of these cases, the individual was telling the truth but no one wanted to listen. If the felt experience is acknowledged, in a safe and appropriate way, the truth can be felt.

When the truth is spoken, we feel it in our body, we have a resonance with it

We can only face our truth when we are ready. If contemplating it feels overwhelming, we should listen to that intuition and take things slowly, giving ourselves plenty of time to come to terms with things. We don't have to do any of this inner work until it feels right, and we might choose to explore this with a trusted practitioner for extra support. There are no 'musts' or 'shoulds' here. Honouring ourselves is deciding what is right and best for us right in the here and now. Nonetheless, we can be curious about this fear of overwhelm and what that may carry. Finding the right time and space to explore our truth is part of the healing process and we will find our way to this if we want to.

Spiral of Learning

Connect with your body, by doing some deep breathing exercises, settling yourself so you feel calm and centred. See the Spiral of Learning for the previous chapter for help in this. Then sit with the question: What is my truth?

See what comes up from within rather than repeating any old stories or narratives that you are familiar with. See if you can make a connection with your felt experience. If it feels too much, or you feel blank, just respect that, don't fight it or dishonour it; just observe and perhaps note in your journal whatever it is you are feeling.

The questions for us all to consider is: "What have I been saying no to, that I now want to say yes to, today? Can I feel that resounding YES in my body, in my felt experience? Whose help might I need to answer these questions? What is the first next step on the road to saying YES to myself?"

CHAPTER 21
How to Create a Healthy Caretaker Relationship

Many of us have assumed caretaker roles of rescuer, protector, parent, being dutiful, and organiser as ways of seeking a connection with our mother. These entanglements have grown from our early relationship with her and through distressing life events. We may take up similar roles with others we are close to or within our work. We never made a clear decision to do this, it was how our relationship was programmed. Now we can stand back, reflect and decide how we want to relate from now on.

If this has been our pattern, we may find ourselves increasingly drawn in if our mother is ill for any length of time or ageing and needs help. Alternatively, we may switch from a healthier pattern to an entangled caretaking one if our anxiety about losing her is activated. Daughters with mothers who have problems with alcohol or mental illness may have been caretaking all their lives; others have taken up a caretaking role in response to a mother who appears unable to run her own life or who demands caretaking from her daughter. Entangled caretaking relationships are co-dependent in nature, that is we are both relating to each other through our adapted child, part of our trauma response.

A feature of such relationships is that we are vulnerable to being hurt if our 'service' is rejected or if we are criticised. This happens, for example, if we do something to help our mother, and she pushes us away or ignores our help. Our 'adapted child' has invested so much in this distorted love that such rejections go deep.

The table below reminds us of the difference between an entangled caretaking role and an unentangled one. I have adapted Dr Craig Chalquist's work on co-dependency to illustrate these differences:

Entangled relationship	Healthy Relationship
Rescuing, protecting, being the parent, rejecting, IS the relationship	Supporting others is a minor part of the relationship; we can choose not to be a caretaker
Focuses on the other and neglects self-wellbeing	Takes self-wellbeing seriously alongside any support of the other
Feeling responsible for whatever happens to the other	Knows others are responsible for themselves. Can care for another without a sense of taking responsibility for what happens
A pattern of being over-helpful and rescuing in life generally	Caring and supporting someone when they genuinely need it rather that to serve our anxiety

Accepts maltreatment from the other as part of the relationship; excuses a mother's behaviour	Refuses to be treated or spoken to in undermining or negative ways
Takes on 'all care' rather than calling in others as needed and appropriate; at a cost to self	Recommends other resources to provide care and helps organise it if appropriate, rather than rushing to rescue
Helps/rescues/protects/ parents out of personal emotional need and fear of abandonment	Helps out of generosity of spirit or love, as is able to love and want oneself and doesn't look to others for that
Carries a belief that 'it will be my turn' with the associated frustration that 'my turn never seems to come'	Relates freely without feeling trapped, obligated or resentful

The difference is that when unentangled, we can stand back and bring our own needs into consideration and make clear choices about the extent to which we want to be involved. When entangled, we just react and enact old habits. Old habits react very quickly to old stimuli, for example, the tone of our mother's voice, or an accusatory look; a belief system of ours then kicks in and old behaviour patterns follow it. We can train ourselves to get better at breaking that circuit of stimulus/response. This involves firstly recognising the trigger, then taking a few deep breaths and letting the instant response go, together with the emotions that are caught up in it. Most of us will not achieve this all of the time, but if we manage it some of the time, we build up our capacity not to be immediately triggered. It is miraculous how something as simple as a deep breath can be so transformative.

It is miraculous how something as simple as a deep breath can be so transformative

One of the indicators that we are caught in the left-hand column is that our energy is often drained, and we may find it hard to accept help from others and to rest. One of the legacies of trauma is that we may experience high levels of anxiety about most things most of the time, and having had that for so long, we take it as normal. This can leave us drained and exhausted. It is helpful to check in with our inner sense of how stressed we feel and use techniques that help us reduce those levels, for example deep breathing, meditation, listening to calming music, or walking in nature. It maybe that we are 'wired' to worry and think about our mother's wellbeing rather than our own. I still have anxiety flashbacks to the days leading up to my mother's death, when I had been a willing caretaker, worrying, *'Did I do enough?'* or *'Did I do the right thing?'* I realise now that this is partly a grief reaction, but I think it also comes out of our entanglement, as if I can't trust myself to have done all I could, given the circumstances at the time; that even then, I wasn't a good enough daughter.

Stepping out of these habits requires us to consider, 'do I want to continue relating in this way?' and 'what function is it serving within me?'. This second question helps us identify the underlying anxieties, fears and magical thinking that may be holding it in place. Picture a mother who is self-centred, demanding a care-taker role of her daughter who has unconsciously taken it on. It can leave the daughter feeling angry and hurt, as nothing she does is ever enough. What holds it in place are our old friends, fear of abandonment, the hope that one day it will be different and want-ing any connection with her mother, however dissatisfying. There may also be guilt at the thought of stepping away and fear that her mother would collapse if the pattern didn't continue in this way. Another daughter may find herself in a similar situation, as a pro-tective rescuer to her mother. Her mother depends on her while not taking responsibility for her own life decisions. The daughter may have deep sympathy for her mother and the life she had and carries the burden of her mother's life choices in the past. Part of the daughter's motivation is driven to make amends for her mother's suffering. Her mother has shifted that burden from her-self to her daughter, who has willingly carried it up to now. The daughter may come to recognise that this relationship is not work-ing for her, that it is draining her energy and stopping her living her own life fully. If she digs a bit deeper, she may find that part of her doesn't believe that her mother is capable of running her own life – hence the rescuing. Maybe this is her mother's deepest fear, which she has unconsciously transferred to her daughter.

It can feel as if there are only two options – continue as things are or walk away and abandon her. We can be so caught up in the entanglement that we can't think of an alternative. We always have choices. Even when we are entangled, parts of us are making the choice to relate in that way. We can deny this and say, *"I have no choice,"* but that isn't true. Making different choices might be challenging and might have consequences that need managing, but they are always there as options. We just stop considering what they might be. It is our fear that keeps us entangled, often understandably so.

We always have choices

We can identify that the relationship isn't working for us as it is and decide that due to our mother's needs, we are willing to take on a healthy caretaking role towards her. In doing so we can make a conscious decision after thinking it through. The elements of such a role are in the right-hand side of the table at the beginning of this chapter. In relating in this way, we are careful not to be driven by our adapted child, to give space to ourselves so we can reflect and respond differently. The more we are able to honour and resource ourselves, the better placed we will be to do this. The challenge is to catch when we edge back to the 'saviour' role and when our old habits resurface, with the exhaustion and possibly resentment that comes with it. We have to remind ourselves we are not being selfish considering our needs and looking after ourselves when we put boundaries in place around the time and extent to which we are willing to be involved.

Small Steps Towards Healthy Caretaking

Once you have decided this is what you are committed to doing, for your own wellbeing, you can help ourselves in a number of ways:

Remember she won't change: changing our behaviour will not miraculously change hers; she is likely to continue to want to entangle us, maybe continue wanting to make us feel bad or guilty. When she does this, take a deep breath and settle yourself. We can make a commitment not to take the bait. If we are honouring and resourcing ourself, we do not have to take on board her comments. If she criticises us or makes judgements about us, we can just let them go. Practise letting them bounce off you.

Get skilled at recognising the triggers: we can get better at recognising what activates our habitual responses and learn how to break the cycle by responding differently. This will involve deliberately slowing down our responses putting more space between the trigger and our response, to give us time to think about if and how we want to respond. We won't achieve this all the time, but if we manage it some of the time, we build up our capacity not to be immediately triggered.

Decide, set and keep boundaries: we need to decide what we are prepared to do and not do. In relation to what we 'don't want to do', who else could fulfil that aspect? (For example, maybe a family member or a paid helper if money allows?) If we have siblings, what are they prepared to do and not do? Often the childless or single daughter steps in, colluding with the idea that their siblings 'are too busy'. The daughter in this situation needs to honour her choices and not shoulder the burden singlehandedly. It is important to recognise that we can bring in other resources to support our choices and boundaries. Using our creative thinking will help us do this, including talking with trusted friends and getting their ideas.

Decide how it can work best for you: you may decide to visit for a short time, or you both go out, or you phone at the best time of day/week for you. You may decide to visit her monthly – think through what will work best, put it in practice, and then assess if it was better. If it doesn't work as well as you hoped, try something else. We need to decide, act and evaluate without berating ourselves if it doesn't always work. Resource yourself as much as you can before the encounter so that you are in a good space inside ready to manage any stressors her behaviour may activate. If you know staying for several nights is too much, don't do it. If you want to visit her for that time, think about staying somewhere else, for example, in a B&B if money allows. This gives you breathing space.

Challenge old beliefs: when old thoughts arise, like being selfish or feeling guilty or that we are responsible for our mother's life decisions, recognise them as coming from the 'there and then'. Guilt is something we may have internalised from what are often societal expectations: that the daughter must look after the mother, or that there is something wrong with us if we don't appear to be a loving daughter. It is not acceptable that anyone should sacrifice their own lives and wellbeing for another's. Feeling guilty is akin to feeling responsible and is part of what has kept the entangled relationship in place. The more you can resource yourself, love and care for yourself, the more resilient you will be to those old stimuli.

Responsibility: if part of the caretaker role you have assumed means you have taken on responsibility for certain factors concerning her health, be clear what you *really* can be responsible for and what you can't. You can't for example, ensure she always takes medication other than standing over her. If she forgets, she forgets, it isn't your fault. If she falls, that is distressing but not your fault. We must remember that ultimately, we are not responsible for her decisions. Be attentive to feeling responsible for things you can't be responsible for.

Let go of resentment: if you have decided to take on a caretaking role, do so without expecting gratitude. If some comes your way, great, take it. Resentment is a sign that we haven't set out boundaries firmly enough in response to thinking through what works for us. If you feel it, check in with yourself in case you are slipping back into old patterns.

Alternative interventions: if we find ourselves thinking we *have* to make all the decisions even when our mother has the mental capacity to do that, we can observe that tendency within ourselves and make a different response. I find coaching questions can be useful in these situations. These are open questions – that is they can't be answered by 'yes' or 'no', and so require the daughter to find her own answers. Here are a few examples:

"What help would you like here?"

"What would help you decide/manage this?"

"What would you like to do?"

"How might you make that happen?"

"What thoughts have you had about that?"

If we experience our mother as frustrating, and acting in ways we think are wrong or ill advised, we have a few choices. Trying to convince her to change her ways usually fails and just adds to the frustration. However, we can voice our opinion something along the lines of, *"If it was me, I would make a different decision,"* or *"what outcome are you wanting from this decision?"* What we shouldn't do is step into an argument about it and feel responsible for the outcome. I have talked before about developing skills in having different conversations, many of us will be helped by doing that.

Expectations: we can notice if we are projecting, that is putting onto another, motivations or expectations that don't exist or that we have created. We can notice and question these and ask, *"Am I setting up a stimulus/response habit by assuming something is meant to be, which may not be the case?"* If we have a tendency to do this, we can end up feeling hurt or saddened by something we have almost certainly 'made up' or which doesn't exist, (but which no doubt has resonance with the past). If we let go of projecting our expectations onto another, it changes how we feel about ourselves and our relationships. It liberates us from unrealistic expectations, and we become less frustrated, resentful and angry.

Control: we can help ourselves by differentiating between our control needs and situations that need controlling. For example, we can assess whether or not she is putting herself at risk of actual harm, or if she is merely contemplating something but may not act on it. Part of my control response with my mother was to off-set my anxiety about any given situation. So, I told my elderly mother not to allow anyone to admit her to hospital without my being there. I should add that she was of sound mind. At the end though, she was advised to go to hospital, and was able to decide for herself that this was the sensible thing to do. Can we differentiate between our mother's real needs and our need to be in control?

Listening: this may be challenging as many of us may have stopped listening to our mothers, or only listen out for things that hurt us. The more we can be calm and resourced when with our mother, the better for us but also it has the potential of transmission to her. We know that nervous systems relate to each other, person to person, so if we are agitated then that can mirror agitation she may feel. Similarly, if we are calm this may help her feel calmer. Listening means attending to the other person, being present with them. It doesn't mean we have to agree or disagree or give solutions. It just means we are sitting with her, calmly, when she talks. Perhaps no one has ever really listened to her. Don't expect miracles but calmly listening without rising to any bait may help you fulfil the caretaker role you have taken on.

Space, rest and resourcing yourself: I have said this already several times and I think it worth restating – we need to keep space for us to play, rest and resource ourselves. We can't change patterns if we are either caretaking or working, our energies get too depleted, we can't observe ourselves, reflect and decide how to be with our mother.

We need to recognise that we can only make life healthier for ourselves

None of us need to be a hero to pain. We always have the option not to engage, and we can achieve that from a grounded honouring place in ourselves. It is okay if daughters decide not to have contact with their mother because her behaviour continues to be damaging to their wellbeing. Sometimes it is essential to break the web, to regroup away from the habitual stimulus/response process.

None of us needs to be a 'hero to pain'

Moving out of entanglement may also allow the emergence of grief that has been hidden by our behaviour for years. The grief comes from not being understood or 'met' by our mother, of not having that emotional connection we longed for. When we allow this grief to be present, and feel compassion for ourselves, it becomes easier to move away from the tangled web that entraps us. We can be witness to our own suffering from 'there and then'. We can normalise the grief, rage and other emotional states we have carried from childhood, accepting that they are entirely understandable given our experiences and the context for our growing up. They don't make us a bad person and we don't need to be blamed or apologise for feeling them. They are part of our lived experience, and we can welcome them. It might sound counter-intuitive to welcome these and other parts into our life; you may think this gives them more power to overwhelm you, but that isn't what happens (unless your internal self-hatred attacks you and, if it does, try to notice that that is happening). Instead, open up to your lived experiences and accept them as part of your journey; pause, and take some deep breaths, and remind yourself that whatever you were feeling is understandable. It is okay to feel these things. When we do this, the power of our lived experiences over our 'here and now' reduces, our feelings become softer and less threatening to us. It is the striving to repress them, disown them and then manage how they continue to operate in our life that causes us the suffering and exhaustion.

Helping us step out of the entanglement are the qualities of self-compassion, honouring ourselves and maybe feeling com-passion for our mother. These qualities are addressed in the fol-lowing chapters. As we move forward, we can build up our inner healthy resources and begin to 'stand down' the adapted parts of us from the 'there and then'.

Spiral of Learning

Go back to the Small Steps list, and under each of the headings create a 'To Do' list of small changes you want to make to support your moving out of entanglement:

Remember she won't change	Let go of resentment
Recognise triggers	Alternative interventions
Decide, set and keep boundaries	Expectations
Challenge old beliefs	Control
Responsibility	Listening
Space, rest and resourcing yourself	

Notice which steps are the ones you want to focus on, or where you may have more to do. Choose one and imagine yourself taking the actions. Do the same for another one. Note down how it feels and any other thoughts that arise.

If these actions involve your mother, write the story of how you would enact the actions you have set out. Or you could write the story of a woman, like you, who is behaving in these new ways. Image the interaction and dialogue she would love with her mother perhaps giving some insight into how the woman may be feeling and bringing the scene to a positive outcome for her.

Bring to mind a relationship you have that feels healthy and unentangled, either in the past or the present. List out the components of that relationship – that is, what is present that ensures it is healthy? Relate that to a relationship that doesn't feel so healthy at the moment – what is missing in it? What might be your part in this? Might you be compensating for it in other ways?

One of the characteristics of someone with a history of entanglement, is that we often don't seek help and don't take it when offered. This might be that we are in denial about needing help, or that we don't trust those who purport to help us, or that we have a kind of 'heroic' mentality that we can do everything. Alternatively, we might look for someone to rescue us, and so entangle others. If you recognise this in yourself and want to move beyond entangled relationships, now is the time to recognise your programme patterns and shift your channels of thinking. Seek out the right help for you.

CHAPTER 22
Engaging Compassion and Exploring Forgiveness

Compassion

OED: Compassion, noun: the feeling or emotion when a person is moved by the suffering or distress of another

The Oxford English Dictionary suggests that compassion is evoked by the feelings you get when you see the suffering or distress of another, but it is also important and entirely possible to feel compassion for the suffering you have experienced yourself. So, begin now to connect with a sense of compassion for yourself and all that you have experienced. What does it feel like and how does it show itself in your body (do you feel tearful, anxious, shocked...)? How do you experience this feeling of compassion for others? What happens in your body? Many of us find it much harder to feel compassion for ourselves than others but developing healthy compassion for ourselves is part of honouring our lived experience – every bit of it. Without self-compassion, our ability to learn from our personal reflections is constrained, as we tend to be full of judgement or criticism of ourselves.

Compassion for others, including our mother is part of developing wisdom. This is our ability to recognise that she too has suffered and that her behaviour is an expression of her own emotional trauma. In so doing, we can still hold her responsible for any behaviour that hurt or harmed us, but first, we need to develop self-compassion, by which I mean processing our emotional trauma before we take a step towards feeling compassion for those who may have hurt us. Without that, we are in danger of betraying ourselves, that is, denying or dismissing our hurt to focus on the hurt of others. Wisdom is about holding the whole truth, not only selected parts of it.

Compassion for others, including our mother is part of developing wisdom

In this chapter, I am expanding on the OED definition of compassion. When I use the word compassion I mean: *'emotionally witnessing, without judgement, the pain and suffering that exists in ourselves and others.'* 'Emotionally witnessing' means having some emotional connection with that suffering, being moved and affected but not overwhelmed by it.

It is important to recognise that as children, such emotional witnessing can overwhelm us, and our feelings of compassion can morph into survival mechanisms, that we enact to mitigate our emotional trauma – and it is highly likely these feelings stay with us into adulthood. Such feelings might include:

- Feeling a drive to help others which becomes rescuing or protecting
- Feeling anger and pain on behalf of someone else, through identifying with the suffering of the other while sacrificing ourselves
- Feeling pity for others or ourselves

We can see how easy it is to remain in entanglements unless we can differentiate these processes from compassion. If compassion comes to feel burdensome, then it is not compassion. Neither is it compassion if we jump to feeling responsible and act on that impulse. Conversely, compassion may take us into the service of others within a non-entangled relationship.

Healthy compassion is when we are able to let go of judgement and any associated emotions, and instead, just observe the reality of a given situation and its impact. When applied to ourself, compassion without judgement brings feelings of kindness and self-worth. When, in our self-reflections, we feel anxiety, frustration, exasperation, or when we recognise that we haven't behaved well, if we are able to observe these feelings without judgement, we can begin to unravel the entanglements and look at the reasons behind our feelings. Self-compassion is a gentle loving of ourselves.

The primary task in terms of reclaiming ourselves, is to develop our capacity for self-compassion. When we are better able to do this, then we can explore the extent to which being compassionate to our mother's suffering feels possible. We start through our self-reflections, noting how we treat and think about ourselves, how much we can engage without judgement and what happens when we don't. Suspending judgement through self-compassion helps us learn about ourselves.

Self-compassion is a gentle loving of ourselves

Compassion for our mother is about seeing her as a whole person, disentangling our adapted child from our relationship with her. We don't need to rescue or protect her from her history or her choices, but we can recognise the suffering she has endured as a human in this world. If we can do this, we may feel a warmth towards her that we couldn't feel before and something can soften within us. It doesn't change the hurt we experienced from her behaviour, but we can come to know that it wasn't our fault. That can be freeing. To hear about our mother's story, we may need to ask her and listen quietly, giving her the space to talk.

This is an illustration of how we might be able to engage healthily rather than through the old patterns of our adapted child. If we feel this compassion and warmth, that will be felt by our mother, who may be able to talk more authentically to us about her background. She may soften a bit too. Perhaps no one in our mother's life had ever asked her about what life was like for her, and then listened carefully to the answers. Not all mothers will be able to engage in this way and we need to accept that.

Seeing our mother's suffering is not about denying our own. The two can both be present. Often, we can get caught in a competitive thought, a *'hers was worse than mine so I shouldn't feel what I feel'* scenario; but no one's history trumps another's. They co-exist. If we can be open to our mother's experience as a child or later, it brings the possibility of understanding why she is as she is. It reinforces the sense that her behaviour is not about us and we no longer need to keep believing it is. Developing compassion for my mother's suffering took some years and was helped by therapeutic work which enabled me to understand that my experience hadn't started with me and wasn't about me. In doing this, it allowed me to listen to my mother more attentively, and I witnessed her story and emotions. I was able to be present as her adult daughter.

Feeling compassion for our mother's suffering can enable us to recognise that she is subject to her fate while also recognising that she remains responsible for her actions. The more we know about her background and what she had to endure, the more we may feel compassion for her. We can use our imagination to connect with the possible impacts on her, emotionally. Daughters who have talked of their mother's stories have highlighted many times the grim reality of their history. From them, we have heard of early lives of extreme poverty, maybe lost in the number of siblings, perhaps having been abandoned, or living with violence, alcoholic parents or those who took their own lives; or being shamed and ridiculed for her colour or disability. We can feel compassion for the women who experienced this.

Sometimes even thinking about compassion for someone who has hurt us is profoundly challenging. This is especially true of those who have been physically or sexually abused. Being able to feel compassion for a perpetrator is not essential to disentanglement and healing; but feeling compassion for oneself for having experienced such trauma is. The effects of sexual abuse go deep and are long-lasting, and often unprocessed by those who have experienced them because just the very act of speaking about it is extremely traumatic. Consequently, many never talk of it or get therapeutic help to work through the lasting impact on them. But getting this help is the primary task of disentanglement. Hard as it undoubtedly is, we need to do what we can to process our experience, or it will continue to have a deep and harmful impact on our lives and relationships. Compassion for the suffering the abuser may have experienced as a child is unlikely to be a helpful step in the healing process *until* we have done a lot of work on our own emotional trauma. As we work on ourselves, we can learn that we were not to blame and it wasn't about us, but that we were the victim of the abuser, who needs to carry all responsibility for their actions. In the Resources section I have included a link to Dr Jessica Taylor's work and programmes for victims of physical and sexual abuse.

Sometimes developing compassion for others is just too hard and that's okay. We don't have to go there and we certainly don't have to blame ourselves if authentic compassion is not forthcoming. But we do need to be careful not to slip into, *"They couldn't help it"* type of thinking instead. They could help it, they had choices like we all do – they are not the victim in our story. They may be the victim in their backstory, but not in ours.

Spiral of Learning

One of the exercises around compassion that I found helpful as part of a retreat I was on a few years ago goes as follows:

- *Bring an image of your mother to mind*
- *Say out loud, as if you are saying it to her "I see how you have suffered and that you've experienced pain and fear in your life. I see that your life hasn't turned out the way you might have wanted or anticipated. May you find the love you need. May you find the healing you need."*

If you do this, notice what feelings arise within you. Notice them with compassion. Maybe you notice you didn't want to do the exercise, or can't say the words, or that you feel angry or guilty or numb. Be okay with whatever you experience, feel kindly towards yourself. Use it to develop compassion for yourself.

Another exercise from the Buddhist tradition, is to bring someone to mind and say,

"May you be happy. May you be safe. May you be free from suffering". This can be particularly useful with those who we are finding difficult to feel compassion. Again, it isn't about 'doing' anything just engaging our capacity for compassion.

Remember there is no implied virtue in being able to feel compassion for others who have hurt you. It doesn't signal anything negative about you if you can't engage with such compassion. It may be you never will or just not right now.

Forgiveness

OED: Forgive (verb): to stop feeling angry with someone who has done something to harm, annoy or upset you

Many people believe they 'should' be able to forgive a person who has hurt them, and they feel bad when they can't. Many believe that to forgive someone means we no longer hold them responsible for their actions. If they are adults, that is problematic as we are all responsible for our actions, no matter what history we have.

Forgiving someone can mean, *'I no longer carry this inner fight with you'*; this isn't saying that the person necessarily deserves to be forgiven for what they have done, simply that the one who is forgiving no longer wishes to feel embattled or in a dispute. Neither does this diminish our own experience of the harmful effects of their behaviour; nor excuse them from their responsibility. It simply means that the victim wants to stop feeling angry. Therefore, forgiveness is about the health of the one who is forgiving, not that of the perpetrator. This is the key to forgiveness.

Some people talk of forgiveness leading to compassion; for me it is the other way round. Compassion comes first. Moving beyond the entanglement comes through honouring and developing compassion for ourselves and witnessing the suffering of others without excusing or denying their behaviour.

Being able to forgive is undoubtedly helpful if we wish to step beyond emotional trauma and its impact, and many therapies set forgiveness as the aim. But this can be problematic as sometimes the individual feels they 'have to forgive' when they aren't ready to forgive, or don't want to forgive because their pain is too great.

Dr Jessica Taylor, who talks widely on victim-blaming in relation to sexual and physical abuse, is clear that we don't have to forgive anyone who has abused us, and we shouldn't be pressurised into doing so. To be able to forgive is often seen as a virtue, in that if we are able to forgive, we are a better person for it; and women are often expected to forgive more than men. This puts us under pressure and can make us believe that we have failed if we don't feel forgiveness, thus blaming ourselves when in fact the person who harmed us is responsible.

If we say in respect of our mother: *"I forgive her, she had a tough life"* but then say, *"so I will keep protecting, rescuing and parenting her,"* we will remain forever entangled. We aren't free. This is also true if we think, *"If I say I forgive her, maybe at last I will get the love I want?"* Sometimes the person who has hurt us asks, *"Will you forgive me, I tried my best?"* They probably did try their best – most parents do within their own trauma state – but this may be an invitation to stay entangled through a rescuing form of forgiveness. Similarly, survival forgiveness – continually forgiving another's inappropriate actions as a way of staying in a relationship with them – often means we never get to process our own emotions about that which needs forgiving. We can help ourselves by being mindful of how we think about and use the term 'forgiveness', and what beliefs we carry about it. Forgiveness can only be freely given, not asked for or taken. Forgiveness is a choice to no longer carry a hurt and because it is us who carries the hurt – not the perpetrator. We can only do this if and when we are ready to.

Forgiveness is a choice to no longer carry a hurt

Reconciliation may be an easier way to consider how a relationship where harm has been enacted by one person on another, might be emotionally processed. This isn't about accepting the other's version of events, but about having an honest, truthful conversation about the impact of their behaviour on us, and of them owning their own behaviour and the hurt they caused. For example, if a mother says to her daughter, *"I recognise now that my narcissism had a deep impact on you as a child; I couldn't see you and I know I didn't love you as fully as you needed. My concerns and needs were always uppermost for me, and I know now that meant that yours got lost and I regularly failed to meet them,"* this would be an invitation for some kind of reconciliation between the mother and daughter. Unfortunately, it is rare that someone with a narcissistic survival strategy can come to such realisations, but this kind of statement from a parent recognises the impact of their actions. A daughter may then be able to reconcile her feelings by saying, *"Your behaviour hurt me often and I have carried that all my life; it reverberates through me. I recognise it was tough for you, but the impact on me was considerable."'* Or *"When you hit me, it really hurt physically and emotionally. You pulled my hair in your rage. I have carried that through my life. I get it was hard for you..."* While this kind of conversation carries the potential for some reconciliation, it isn't a process of forgiveness. Reconciliation is about truth sharing and respecting, even when the truth of the other is hard to hear. It is about being open to the suffering of the other, including suffering we might have caused by our fight to be ourselves.

Talking about reconciliation in this way is to identify what might be possible but often isn't. I am including it to illustrate the difference between reconciliation and simple forgiveness. Many of us believe that our mothers are not capable of having those feelings or that kind of conversation, and this may be an accurate assessment. It doesn't mean though, that we can't claim our own truth for ourselves, and that includes the ability to forgive. There is no point blaming our mother for not being able to meet us in that way; if she could, she would. But if we can let go of our longing for resolution or retribution, we can move away from any entanglement. Families do sometimes go to Family Therapy or Family Reconciliation in order to have a safe space to talk about their experience of and with each other, but this isn't currently a very widespread process, and sadly, there are not many practitioners in this field.

In her book, *The Apology*, Eve Esner (now known mononymously as V) focuses on her relationship with her abusive father. Her mother gets little mention other than that she colluded with her father and wasn't able, or failed, to protect her daughter. The daughter had developed an entangled relationship with her father early on in life, looking for love and attachment. He went on to emotionally and physically abuse her in very cruel ways. In this book, she imagines her father is writing his apology and account of himself to her, in which he attempts to feel what she must have felt, to feel his own deep remorse for causing that hurt, taking responsibility for his actions and doing the work needed to understand why he did what he did. He explores his own history and starts off using this as an excuse, but he comes to recognise that he is failing to take responsibility for the pain he inflicted on her. He comes to understand that he has to own his shame and that he cannot ask for the forgiveness of his daughter, as that is about entangling her. It is a powerful book about apology and reconciliation, and I recommend it. Esner wrote the book as she knew no apology would be forthcoming from her father, so she used her imagination to speak for him. It was her way of breaking an emotional entanglement and her longing for acknowledgement.

The issues about forgiveness and reconciliation also apply to us and any behaviour we have enacted that has hurt or harmed others. We need to take responsibility for that; we can't just ask for forgiveness or say; *"I'm sorry."* We need to say something like, *"I recognise that my actions have hurt you. I can imagine how that must have felt and how that continues within you. I failed you at a time you needed me, as I was caught up in my own life. I deeply regret what I did to you."* However, this has to be said without any expectation that it will produce reconciliation or as a step to asking for forgiveness. We need to do it as part of honouring ourselves, otherwise it becomes manipulative and invokes further entanglement. We don't have the right to ask for forgiveness. If it brings reconciliation, that is all well and good. If it doesn't, we need to bear that.

That said, we never need to apologise for our behaviour as children, so if ever our mothers expect us to apologise for being a 'difficult child' or for 'causing her pain' or 'being obstructive' don't get sucked into this survival web. It is part of the inverted victim dynamic, where the child who is the victim is portrayed as the perpetrator. It is victim blaming. However, in the spirit of reconciliation, we may need to be open to feedback from our mother about how our behaviour as adolescents and adults affected her.

We never need to apologise for our behaviour as children

Spiral of Learning

The first step is to assess within yourself if you are ready to engage with compassion for your mother. If you are not, just note down in your Reflective Diary what is getting in the way and what, if anything, you may want to do to process those things you have identified. Then note down how you may want to do that and when.

Focus on your capacity to feel compassion for yourself. Write a letter to yourself, expressing this compassion and love, and thanks to those adapted internal parts that helped you survive

If it feels right, write a letter of apology from a mother like yours to her daughter. Imagine the mother setting out her story, background, her emotional landscape and what might have been happening for her, then taking responsibility for her actions towards her daughter.

What emotions arose for you as you wrote this letter? Has anything shifted for you in relation to how you feel towards your mother?

What would forgiveness mean for you? Maybe write for 15 minutes about this in your journal allowing different views and thoughts to come up.

CHAPTER 23
Becoming Our Own Good Enough Loving Mother (More of the Time)

The original title for this chapter didn't have 'good enough' or (more of the time) added to it. I was struggling to write these final words in the way I wanted to, and through discussion with a colleague, I realised I had been setting myself, and readers, an impossible target. Donald Winnicott, who I have referred to before, offered the concept of the 'good enough mother' to release mothers from the impossible expectations placed on them. I certainly do not want to compound this by placing impossible expectations on ourselves, so I have therefore added 'good enough' and (more of the time) to release us from that expectation. If we can just love ourselves unconditionally (as a good mother would) a bit more of the time, we are honouring ourselves and that is good enough. This is an achievable aim. We do it a bit at a time, repeatedly over time. In that way, we learn how to do be our own good enough loving mother more of the time.

But first, we need to differentiate loving ourselves from narcissism. One is healthy, the other is an expression of emotional trauma. Loving ourselves is to be self-caring, to protect ourselves, to look out for and guide ourselves through the undergrowth of this honouring path we are on. Narcissism is about making ourselves centre stage in our life, to the detriment of everyone else, believing that others are just actors in our life, there to meet our needs. One of the challenges in talking about loving ourselves, for any of us who are not so good at that, is that we return to these conditioned fears of being selfish and self-centred. Loving ourselves is neither of these.

Some of us may already have an internalised sense of loving and caring for ourselves that came from our actual loving mother. Celebrate that. The rest of us are spread out along the spectrum of never having felt a sense of love for ourselves to feeling it all the time. If we didn't get unconditional love from our mother, we might still have been able to feel some elements of unconditional love and maternal caring from others, not always female. For some, it might have been an aunt, father, uncle, grandparent, a foster or step-parent, a close friend of the family, the mother of a friend, or a teacher. Some may have experienced this kind of support from a therapist. Where we have such experiences, perhaps we can feel our way back to what this felt like, so that we can sense what we are seeking to replicate for ourselves.

Developing our own loving mother and carrying her within us may require effort and commitment for some of us. Maybe we have carried a negative 'mother' voice or attitude within us for so long, it has become pervasive and highly active in our life. We can start by just noticing that in our self-reflections. If we haven't inter-nalised our own loving mother, we may look for 'her' in a partner or in a child (neither necessarily female). This inevitably brings entanglements as we are putting onto others the requirement that they meet our unmet child needs for love. Developing our own internal loving mother is therefore important for our other relationships and not only for ourselves.

It may be that in becoming a mother yourself, you have located a different place within you that is able to give unconditional love to your child, respecting their individuality while providing gentle emotional holding and guidance. Those of us who are not mothers, by choice or not, may have found ways to engage our capacity for mothering others, without rescuing them. Maybe that is through step-children, nephews and nieces, children of friends or through charitable work. There are many ways to express our nurturing selves. Being unable to be a loving mother to ourselves doesn't mean that we can't make a good shot at being that for another.

Developing our own internal loving mother is therefore important for our other relationships and not only with ourselves

If we can experience this loving maternal connection with another, are we more able to do the same for ourselves? The answer is not always. We may need to patiently nurture and grow this love for ourselves over time. As you would expect, this can also bring its challenges as our old patterns and beliefs are ever ready to block such progress. Developing our own loving mother is closely associated with honouring, reclaiming and resourcing ourselves, and once we have initiated these processes, we will find that we are more caring and compassionate to ourselves. Loving connection is not just a warm feeling, but a capacity to guide ourselves sensitively through our lives in a way that honours us and others. This guidance has wisdom; a depth to it that comes from our self-reflection and engagement with our felt experience, from our emerging conscious awareness. It is the opposite of the impulse constantly to make decisions, of always managing and organising or planning. Unconditional love is compassion and care for ourselves, *especially* when we think we have messed up or got caught in old patterns.

Loving connection is not just a warm feeling, but a capacity to guide ourselves sensitively through our lives in a way that honours us and others

Wherever we put ourselves on the Spectrum of Honouring discussed at the beginning of this section, it is now possible to decide what action we are prepared to take that will move us gradually along from where we start to the 'fully loving ourselves' end. We do have to discover for ourselves how to achieve this by noticing what facilitates our loving connection and what impedes it – there is no fixed path to success. Certainly, slowing down helps, as does rest and quiet periods of reflection. If we are tired or exhausted a lot of the time, my experience tells me this will make the task much harder. So slow down and be kind to yourself.

We are likely to find many resources – that initially we may never have considered, or may even reject out of hand – that will help us on this journey, including a highly tuned intuition, the motivation to bring more calm and lively energy to our lives, and the courage to face what has been absent in ourselves. I am doing what I can to move slowly along this spectrum so that I can be my own good enough mother (most of the time). I have made progress, which I can see when I read back through my reflective journals. The challenge when writing about this journey is to put the concept of our own (good enough) loving mother into words, as it is a felt sense, not one we can come to analytically. We feel it in our bones, and it is that feeling that steadies and guides us.

Here, I have found some words that I hope will open you to this felt sense, with the intention of giving some shape to the bundle of qualities, behaviour, beliefs and actions that connect with it:

Felt Senses

- Self-compassion
- Self-care and self-love (not narcissistic but unconditional love of ourselves)
- Self-nurturing through good food, rest, and life-enhancing activity
- Self-encouraging, being enthusiastic about our unique resources and contributions
- Having a sense of abundance rather than scarcity
- Having a sense that there is enough love and space for us to be who we are, and that we give ourselves that spaciousness
- Fiercely protective of our life energy; not allowing others to diminish it – like a lioness protecting her cubs
- The capacity to hug and soothe ourselves
- Guiding our lives to fulfil our sense of ourselves
- Recognising what we need for our own well-being

You may feel a new strength when you undertake this work; not a strength as in 'power over' or the 'warrior' but the strength that comes from a sense of being grounded, that is, firmly standing your ground, not easy to push over and not drifting from one thing to the next.

Spiral of Learning

Feel free to make your own list of 'Felt Senses' – ones that are unique to you – to guide you in this process. What will you include? Have a good look at your list when complete – what is your response to each item? Do they feel comfortable or challenging to you?

Where would you put yourself now, on the Spectrum of Honouring? Are you 'not being a loving mother to myself' (and if so, why might that be), or have you begun to be 'a good enough loving mother to myself most of the time'?

- *Which characteristics or resources within this process do you already practise, if any?*
- *Which characteristics or resources do you want to focus on to develop this further?*
- *What comes to mind about how you might achieve that?*
- *Whose help might you need?*

Developing this ability to love, honour and protect ourselves and therefore not to entangle others, is what this book has been about. We have moved through many stages to get to this point of the internalised 'good enough' loving mother. We started by developing our awareness of what is really happening in the present and recognising our part in keeping it going; then we moved into deepening our understanding and insights of these processes. Alongside this has been the invitation to question ourselves, to use self-reflection and reflective journaling to raise our self-awareness and to support our learning. At several points I have referred to the support we might need from the right kind of therapy or other practices and how many of us are programmed not to seek help, or if we do, to entangle the helper as our rescuer. Whatever is present in us is an opportunity to learn something about ourselves, although sometimes we may put up barriers to learning through our defensive self who is still afraid. Whatever our experience is, we can just notice it.

Being affected by emotional trauma isn't a block to our development, nor does it mean something is wrong with us or we are broken. It becomes the focus of our learning and offers us movement towards healing and emotional health. It is, after all, part of the human condition. For some of us, the impact is great in terms of how we try to survive the emotional pain as, unfortunately, our survival responses can do us harm. Where that is the case, skilled professional help is out there waiting to support us in whatever steps to health we may want to take. The great tragedy is that so much of it needs to be paid for by the individual, who often does not have access to financial resources. However, if we are struggling, we can always ask for help and sometimes it comes from the most unexpected quarters; and sometimes the help we need is more affordable than we think, or occasionally, is given to us or is freely available. Others of us can be good friends to those who are finding this movement challenging. We can witness, listen and encourage, without judgement and with compassion, and without rushing to rescue.

There are some final points that I suggest we all hold in mind:
- We all have resources in our healthy Self, no matter how difficult it may feel at times to access them. They are there, waiting for us to find them and then develop them. *Celebrate*

this inner flame that never went out, no matter what your early experience was; it has travelled with you all this time waiting for you to create the conditions in which it can flourish.

- As infants and children what happened to us wasn't our fault. We are not responsible.
- As adults, we are responsible for our part in keeping our suffering going. We should not blame ourselves for this and can recognise that our adapted child was trying to protect us, but has become maladaptive now we are adults.
- Our mother also carries her own pain and suffering. That doesn't excuse how she may have treated us, but it explains it and helps us to remember that it was never about us.
- We can move beyond entangled and difficult relationships, letting go of any anger and resentment that festers within. We must want to do this, and then do the personal work to support that movement. Just wanting isn't enough.
- We can move beyond treating ourselves badly or critically, and from living someone else's version of what our life should be. We can reclaim ourselves and our life.
- We are helped by surrounding ourselves with the company of good women and friends, whatever that means to us.

Spiral of Learning and Change

As you come to the end of this book, take as long as you need or want to sit with what you have taken from it.

- *What are the key 'stand out' things that were helpful to you?*
- *What messages are you taking from your reading and reflections?*
- *What have you learnt that is useful?*
- *How will you apply that learning?*
- *What, if any changes do you notice within yourself and in your relationship with your mother?*

I am always interested to hear what you have taken from this book, so please do let me know. Thank you for reading it, I sincerely hope that it has been valuable to you. **Julia@becomingourselves.co.uk**

Postscript

When I was starting my research for this book, I came across the beginning of a memoir my mother had written in her 80s. I was unable to read it; I feared something in it. In writing this last section, I became more curious about it, and took it out again and read it. A lot of what she had written I knew, and like all memoirs a lot was left out, but I was deeply moved by her story of childhood and her experiences during World War 2. There was little joy or loving kindness to her, other than some men she had relationships with who clearly deeply cared for her. I was full of compassion for her as I read it.

I was left with a deep awareness that she and I were entangled by grief and loss. Our whole family was, from the impact of the war on both my parents, from my mother's early experiences and her mother's before her, and then the death of my father. We had no way between us to work through all that grief, and we had no support.

Like many daughters in this book, my father played a major part in my development, my sense of myself and how I have lived out my life. I haven't focused on fathers, but that is not to imply that many of us were not held lovingly by them or that we carry a wound or wounds from their behaviour and the impact of their trauma. We can be equally entangled with our father and how we carry him within ourselves. However, we can work through that in the same way as we do with our mother.

One daughter said to me, *"I took the good stuff and left the rest."* For a long time, I was not able to take in the good stuff but in writing this book, I have been able to do that more and more as my defences have softened, my perspective has widened, and my honouring of myself has deepened. I wish the same for you.

Julia Vaughan Smith

www.becomingourselves.co.uk
julia@becomingourselves.co.uk

Resources and Bibliography

Resources

https://www.victimfocus.org.uk/ This is headed up by Dr Jessica Taylor, whose book *'Why Women are Blamed for Everything'* gives a comprehensive account of victim blaming. Victim focus supports women who have been sexually or physically abused. It also has some free online programmes.

Taylor, Jessica (2020) *'Why Women are Blamed for Everything'* Lulu.com

http://www.safehandsthinkingminds.co.uk/about-us/ This carries the work of Dr Karen Treisman, an expert in trauma. The website has many very useful resources, some free some not, for calming and resourcing ourselves. She also has resources for children.

Helping our creativity:

'The Artists Way', (2020) Souvenir Press, *'Walking in this World'* (2002) Random House and *'The Right to Write'* (1998) Pan MacMillan Ltd – all by Julia Cameron

'Writing toward Wholeness : Lessons inspired by C. G. Jung' by Susan M Tiberghien, (2018), Chiron Publications. Using Active Imagination exercises to deepen our self-awareness

'Wild Mind' by Natalie Goldberg (1991), Random House. Using writing to support our personal growth.

Co-dependency:

https://jungplatform.com/ 'Co-dependence, How to Identify and Heal' taught by Dr Craig Chalquist.

Trauma Related

Gerhardt, Sue (2004) *Why Love Matters: how affection shapes a baby's brain* Brunner-Routledge

Harris, Massimilla; Harris, Bud (2014) *Into the Heart of the Feminine: Facing the Death Mother Archetype to Reclaim Love, Strength and Vitality.* Daphne Publications

Hübl, Thomas (2019) *Collective Trauma Healing* Sounds True, Colorado

Maté, Gabor (2003) *The Body Says No* Wiley

Maté, Gabor (2008) *In the Realm of the Hungry Ghost* Vintage Canada

Miller, Alice (2001) *The Truth Will Set You Free.* Basic Books

Miller, Alice (2004) *The Body Never Lies: The Lingering Effects of Hurtful Parenting* W.W. Norton & Co

Ruppert, Franz (2014) *Trauma, Fear and Love* Green Balloon Publishing UK

Ruppert, Franz (Ed) (2012) *Early Trauma* Green Balloon Publishing UK

Sieff, Daniela (2015) *Understanding and Healing Emotional Trauma* Routledge

Van der Kolk, Bessel (2014) *The Body Keeps the Score* Allen Lane

Wolynn, Mark (2016 *It didn't start with you* Viking

Woodman, Marion (1985) *The Pregnant Virgin: A Process of Psychological Transformation* Inner City Books

Woodman, Marion (1982) *Addiction to Perfection* Inner City Books

Non-Fiction

Almond, Barbara (2011) T*he Monster Within: The Hidden Side of Motherhood* University of California Press

Block, Dorothy (1979) *So the Witch Won't Eat Me: Fantasy and the Child's Fear of Infanticide* Burnet Books

Chödrön, Prema (1997) *When Things Fall Apart* Thorsons Classics

Eddo-Lodge, Reni (2017) *Why I'm no longer talking about Race* Bloomsbury Publishing

Hartley, Linda (2001) *Servants of the Sacred Dream. Rebirthing the Deep Feminine* Elmdon Books

Lewis, Helen (2020) *Difficult Women: The History of Feminism in 11 Fights* Jonathan Cape, London

Manne, Kate (2018) *Down Girl: The Logic of Misogyny* Penguin Random House UK

Newton Verrier, Nancy (1991) *The Primal Wound: Understanding the Adopted Child* Gateway Press Inc

Parker, Rozsika (1995) *Torn in Two: The Experience of Maternal Ambivalence.* Virago Press London

Woodman, Marion and Mellick, Jill (2000) *Coming Home to Myself: Reflections for Nurturing a Woman's Body and Soul.* Conari Press/ Redwheel SF

Woodman, Marion (1992) *Leaving My Father's House.* Shambala, Boston

Memoir/Autobiography

Brathwaite, Candice (2020) *I Am Not Your Baby Mother.* Quercus

Cumming, Laura (2019) *On Chapel Sands My mother and other missing persons.* Chatto and Windus London

Ensler, Eve (2019) *The Apology.* Bloomsbury

Gleeson, Sinead (2019) *Constellations: Reflections From Life* Picador

Levy, Deborah (2013) *Things I Don't Want to Know* Penguin Random House UK

Orr, Deborah (2020) *Motherwell: A Girlhood.* Weidenfeld & Nicolson

Pine, Emilie (2018) *Notes to Self* Penguin Random House UK

Sissay, Lemn (2020) *My Name is Why* Cannongate Books

Fiction

Carty-Williams, Candice (2019) *Queenie* Trapeze Pub

Henriques, Kate ate (2017) *The Fat Girl in the Kitchen.* Shed Publications

Bennet, Brit (2020) *The Mothers* Dialogue Books

Forster, Margaret (2013) *The Unknown Bridesmaid.* Chatto & Windus

Gunis, Emily (2019) *The Lost Child* THE HEADLINEREVIEW

Westmacott, Mary (aka Agatha Christie) (1952) *A Daughter's a Daughter* Harper Collins (2014)

About the Author

Julia Vaughan Smith M.A, DIHP, has been a successful accredited coach for many years and was a psychotherapist in private practice, latterly focusing on the legacy of emotional trauma. She teaches about coaching and trauma and applied psychotherapy. Her experience as a daughter has also informed her thinking and insights. She is the author of 'Coaching and Trauma: from surviving to thriving' (2019) and 'Therapist to Coach' (2006) both published by Open University Press/McGraw Hill.

Also by the Author

COACHING AND TRAUMA: FROM SURVIVING TO THRIVING

75% of reviewers on Amazon gave this book 5 stars. Here is what some of them said:

"This is a must-read book for all coaches who want to become 'trauma informed', both for themselves and for the benefit of their coaching clients. Julia guides us through a very readable and easy-to-understand explanation of how the 'here and now' of common coaching dilemmas such as imposter syndrome, bullying, stress, burnout, inner critic, stuckness etc can be connected in some way with the 'there and then' of some past trauma."

Yvonne Flynn

"This is a hugely important book. If as a coach you think trauma is off-limits and belongs firmly in the therapeutic world, then please read this"

Zen Reader

"What a brilliantly accessible book for coaches, which is long overdue. The case studies bring the book to life and the final chapter on boundaries, challenges and healing is invaluable to self-reflection and supervision."

Devonian

"The book is so clearly set out and I had no trouble understanding it at all. Not only did it give me an even deeper insight into my own healing but it also helped me understand how to meet the trauma in the client when it surfaces."

Olivia O'Shea.

THERAPIST INTO COACH

"This book has been on the recommended reading list of my EMCC Global Therapist to Coach Senior Practitioner in Coaching Programme for many years. Crucially, it contains a valuable chapter on the traps therapists can fall into when they get 'stuck' as a coach and fall back into a therapeutic mode"

Dr Trish Turner, Managing Director
Therapist to Coach Ltd

"I found the book engaging right from the start where Julia describes the potential reasons and motivations for therapists to move towards coaching. I felt almost uncomfortably seen, as if she knew what was going on in my mind. There is something about Julia's understanding of her target audience, and the relational way in which it is written, that made it much easier for me to stay focused. I found the examples of coaching conversations very helpful in demonstrating how therapy and coaching do differ, complimenting the chapter that explicitly describes the key differences. This is essential reading for therapists who are moving towards coaching."

Amanda Williamson, Coach and Counsellor

Milton Keynes UK
Ingram Content Group UK Ltd.
UKHW050716030424
440471UK00008BA/88